LOU AND EUSTACE

PAT BACKLEY

CONTENTS

ACKNOWLEDGMENTS

As always, I dedicate this book to
my beloved daughter, Lucy.

I would also like to thank my wonderful editor, Colleen
Ward. It seems we have become a great team!

This is the second book in my ANCESTORS series.
Although these books are fictional, many of the
people and events mentioned in them are real.

Without my ancestors, without all the people who
lived before me, there would be no stories to tell. As
they are now gone and no longer have voices to share
their experiences, I am very proud and honoured to
be the bridge that can tell the tales of their lives.

PREFACE

A SIMPLE FAMILY TREE

It was common in the 19th and early 20th centuries to give male children the same names as their ancestors. For this reason, here is some family genealogy. Hopefully, you will be able to keep up with all the different Arthurs!

> **ARTHUR PLANT married his wife, MABEL, in 1843.**
>
> **Their son, another ARTHUR PLANT (JR.), married JANE SEED in 1879.**
>
> **ARTHUR and JANE'S youngest child, LOUISA (LOU), married EUSTACE IN 1913.**
>
> **Lou's sister Ann also named her son Arthur.**

SOUTHWARK, LONDON, 1913
LOU'S WEDDING DAY

"Come on Lou, get a move on! He may be head over heels about you, but that'll soon wear off if you keep him hanging around too long!"

"Yea, hurry up Lou, it's blooming freezing sitting here on the stairs. Just open the door, we all want to see you."

"What's up, can't you fit into it or something?"

Louisa Ann Plant smiled to herself as she admired her reflection in the cracked, old mirror. She adjusted the pretty flower circlet that was perched on her curly, brown hair- hair that had been freshly washed for the occasion, hair that she had allowed her sisters to wrap in rags last night, to ensure she had beautiful ringlets this morning.

"Okay you lot, stop nagging. I'll be there in a jiffy."

The bedroom door opened and they all gasped in surprise.

"Blimey, Lou, you look like a princess. Not like our grubby little sister at all."

Ann, the eldest of the Plant girls, was genuinely shocked.

Of course they had always known that little Louisa, the much-loved baby of the family, was pretty - probably the prettiest of them all. Until now, however, they hadn't realised just how lovely she really was.

Standing before them in her cream satin wedding gown, holding a pretty little flower posy to match the circlet in her hair, she did indeed look like a princess.

"Oh Lou, you look so beautiful. Wait 'til Mum and Dad see you. I bet Mum will start howling again."

It was a well-known fact that Jane Plant, the girl's mother, was a little prone to tears. Surely today, when the last of her girls was getting married, she was allowed a tear or two.

Jane made it very clear that she could hardly believe her little Louisa was soon going to be a married woman. Wasn't she too young? It seemed like no time had passed since she was born, here in this very house where she donned her wedding dress. This had been over twenty-three years ago, but it seemed like just yesterday!

"What on earth is all that racket going on upstairs? Shouldn't we be getting to the church? We don't want to keep the lad waiting; he's probably nervous enough as it is."

Jane gazed at her love as she spoke, Arthur Plant, her husband of 35 years and the father to their six daughters. Even when she was standing on her tiptoes, she still had to look up to see him.

She knew that secretly, Arthur had always hoped for a son. He wanted someone to carry on the family name but he had never voiced it, never wished it out loud. However, Jane knew him, and had always noticed the rather wistful look on his face when other men were celebrating the birth of their boys.

Despite how much he desired a son, he had greeted the arrival of each new baby girl as if it was the most wonderful thing in the world. And what a marvellous father he had turned out to be! Nothing was ever too much trouble when it came to his girls. Jane knew that Arthur would go to the ends of the earth, or even to the moon, if he thought it would make his wife or daughters happy.

Now here they were, about to marry off the last of their girls. The event was bittersweet; and the thought of letting their littlest one go made them both rather sad. It seemed like just a few years ago that their small house had echoed the sound of all six of their children, laughing and squabbling as sisters do. These had been such happy, glorious years.

Arthur felt tears welling up, and quickly got the clean handkerchief out of his top pocket and blew his nose noisily.

His wife smiled. What an old softy he was.

"Come on, you lot. Hurry up or he'll give up and go home, thinking you're not going to show up."

Of course, the whole house knew that was rubbish. There was no way that Louisa's young man, Eustace, was going anywhere. He worshipped the ground she walked on and would wait in the cold, draughty church for hours if necessary.

Arthur sunk down dramatically into the old, wooden kitchen chair and put his head in his hands.

"What on earth did I do to end up with six girls? Seven, if I include you, my darling. It would be enough to drive even a *sane* man 'round the bend. Sometimes this house is a bit like Bedlam."

He winced as he said this, remembering an old aunty who *had* actually been sent to Bedlam, the old lunatic asylum. She had been a nice, old girl, but when she started losing her mind - getting loud and uncontrollable - she had been admitted to that hell hole. He had only been a young lad at the time, but he could remember being upset while hearing how she cried as they carted her off.

Arthur winced again as he heard all the laughing and shouting coming down the stairs. How could such a quiet chap like himself ever have fathered six glorious, loud, and beautiful creatures? And they were all so different, all with their own unique characters.

Of course, sometimes he called them by the wrong names, but he considered that a bit inevitable when he thought about the names Jane had insisted on giving them.

She had been so young when they got married, his Jane. She was only 18 when they walked down the aisle of the old stone church in Southwark. It had been the same church where all his ancestors, going back two or three hundred years, had been christened, married, and buried. The ancient churchyard was heaving under the weight of all the stone and granite angels bearing the names of his ancestors, the Plants.

When he was just a young lad, back in 1872, his grandfather sat him down and told him the whole family history. He had been in awe, open mouthed as he heard the stories.

His grandfather told stories of green fields, farms, and open countryside, just outside the old city boundaries. The visuals were incomprehensible to him, a lad who was, at the time, growing up close to the River Thames, in the crowded streets of Southwark.

Southwark. The very sound of the name always made him smile. Southwark was Arthur's place - the place that was in his very heart and soul. He knew every step of the city, every nook and cranny.

As a lad, he had spent hours roaming along the banks of the Thames, watching all the activity on the river: the great cargo ships bringing exotic wares from the far-flung corners of the earth, the little fishing boats, the barges. *His* river was a whole world in itself. He had actually never ventured north of the river.

Southwark, on the south side of the River Thames, was enough for him.

He had heard stories, of course, told by people from *the other side*, who were disillusioned enough to think *they* lived in the best place. There was definite rivalry, each group believing their side was best. But Arthur knew the truth. Nowhere in the whole world was better than *his* Southwark.

Looking back, it had been a marvellous place to bring up his girls. They were surrounded on all sides by family. He had never known anything different, and he wanted just the same for his daughters. He had been delighted, once he was married, to remain in the Peabody Buildings on Southwark Street, staying on the very same block where he had grown up.

ARTHUR PLANT

Born at home, in Peabody Buildings, Arthur had been a rather sickly baby. The youngest of twelve children - five of whom had died before they reached their third birthdays of diseases that thrived in the slums - he had been fussed over and cosseted so much that he always believed he was rather special, a *golden* child.

Surprisingly, his older siblings didn't mind his attitude at all; they loved him dearly, their little, golden-haired brother, and were just hoping he wouldn't die just a child like the others.

Although Arthur thought Southwark was the most marvellous place in the world to grow up, in truth, the conditions were harsh and many lived in poverty and anxiety.

The young lad was blessed with a loving family, a family that was determined to overcome any misfortune that life threw at them.

His father, also called Arthur, was a tall, handsome man, a man who had worked hard all his life to support his family. Often he participated in soul-destroying, back-breaking work, but he had done it cheerfully anyway, glad to be able to provide for his family: there was always a decent roof over their heads and food on their table. He was very proud that his little family never went without. They didn't have much, but he had always been able to give his wife, Mabel, enough shillings to buy what she needed every week at Borough Market.

That's where Arthur Sr. had met her, the love of his life, Mabel.

She was from one of the oldest Southwark families - her family tree went back even further than his - and she worked on the market selling whatever fish her brothers managed to catch.

It was slim pickings sometimes, as often, they didn't manage to catch much of anything at all. The River Thames was a difficult mistress, generous at times, but awfully mean at others. However, Mabel's family had fished it for generations, so they were used to the fluctuations of the tides.

Her market stall was always popular. She was such a gregarious person, always willing to take the time to chat to all the old women who hung around the market for hours - those who were whiling away their time rather than going back to their lonely and dismal dwellings.

She followed in the footsteps of generations of strong, hardworking women who had manned the same stall where she stood hawking her wares on the day she and Arthur met. She had started learning her skills when she was just six years old, a willing and able apprentice, keen to learn all the skills the older women in her family could teach her.

Mabel was a Londoner, through and through. An ordinary, yet extraordinary woman, who was fierce and loving in equal measures. She was fierce when defending the people she loved, and loving of almost everybody.

Once they were married, old Arthur realized Mabel had a way of collecting waifs, strays, and anyone down on their luck, so at times it seemed as though their little home was bursting at the seams. They were always trying to accommodate extra bodies she had welcomed there for "a good feed," or "a bed for the night."

Many people thought she was an angel in disguise, his Mabel. To her husband and seven surviving children, she was definitely an angel, there was no doubt about that. They all adored her absolutely.

She was tiny in stature, but huge in personality. At just 4'10" tall, her husband towered over her. Somehow, though, people didn't notice the difference once they got to know her. Her personality was so loud and colourful that in many ways, despite his superior height, her husband Arthur shrunk in comparison - and he was very happy to do so. Although he was incredibly proud of "his Mabel," he was a rather shy, retiring man himself. He was always very happy to hide behind her at social occasions, allowing her to "rule the roost."

All their children adored her, particularly young Arthur.

So, having grown up in such a loving, huge, and rather chaotic family, he felt reasonably well prepared for the rigours of life as a father to six feisty daughters!

BACK TO THE WEDDING
LONDON 1913

"**O**kay, that's enough, you girls! Get down here at once. I'm not waiting any longer. Your mum and grannies are about to head off to the church right now. I'll go with them if you don't hurry up, then Lou will just have to walk there on her own!"

There was a flurry of giggling as the girls came downstairs. It sounded a bit like a herd of baby elephants clomping their way down the old wooden staircase.

"What do you think, Dad? Doesn't she look beautiful?"

For a few moments, Arthur was too choked up to speak as he looked across his daughters towards Lou.

"Oh my darling, you look just like your mum did on our wedding day. So, so beautiful."

The tears fell down his handsome weathered face and he made no attempt to brush them away. He just stood in awe, gazing at his youngest daughter in her wedding dress.

He felt his wife's hand slip gently into his and give it a squeeze. His Jane knew exactly how he was feeling.

After all, hadn't they already given five of their girls away in marriage? And now it seemed they had to part with their last one, their youngest, their little Louisa. It was heartbreaking, but at least she was still going to live nearby. She and Eustace, her husband to be, were going to be moving into the block opposite, in Peabody Buildings. They would be living in the flat where Lou's eldest sister Ann lived with her husband, baby son, and the girls' two grannies.

The two grannies... matriarchs and rocks of the family. They were the two everyone sought for advice, comfort, and the odd loan of a few shillings!

Both now widowed and seemingly ancient, these two old women had more to share than just shillings. They each had stories that would make your hair curl, stories of when they were young and the world was a different place. Their lived history entranced the old and young alike. No one ever tired of listening to either of them.

"Well, I don't know. In my day, we would never have dreamt of keeping the vicar *or* our young man waiting! I just don't know where you young ones get your manners from."

Granny Mabel spoke in her Cockney, fishmonger's accent. She had been born on the south side of the river, but she and all her family - going back many generations - were proud to call themselves Cockneys. Historically, there had always been some debate as to whether "Southerners" could actually classify themselves as real Cockneys; from a very young age, Mabel had heard her old aunties in the fish stall arguing this point:

"Bloody cheek. How dare those stuck-up folk on the other side think they own the title? We're just as Cockney as they are; we can hear the sound of the Bow Bells too!"

As the other old lady standing in the crowded kitchen started to speak, everyone turned to look at her. Her voice was quieter and rather more cultured than Mabel's: "I agree, Mabel, I just hope that lovely young man doesn't get fed up waiting and leave our beautiful girl jilted at the altar."

Granny Ann was as different from Granny Mabel as it was possible to be. Physically speaking, while she too was tiny in stature - both women measured less than five feet tall -where Mabel was stocky with a large bosom and big, strong hands, Ann was petite in every sense of the word.

Granny Mabel was a real London Cockney. She had been born into a loud, flamboyant family - a family of fishermen, sailors, and dockers - and brought up beside the River Thames. Her family was poor and proud. They always worked to support each other and deal with whatever misfortunes life threw at them. They were a family that worked hard, fought hard, and loved hard - a big, noisy, smelly bunch. (Not smelly because they were unclean, smelly because they could never *quite* get rid of the stench of the fish their lives depended on.

Granny Ann on the other hand, was an entirely different kettle of fish. She was quiet, cultured, and rarely spoke out of turn. In fact, she was so quiet that people often forgot she was there, sitting quietly by the fire in the corner of the room, wearing her black, knitted shawl.

Even so, Arthur never took his mother-in-law, Ann, for granted. He knew just how worldly wise she was, how much she had seen in her long life, how much she had suffered. He loved her dearly and would always ensure that she, like his own mum, Mabel, was taken care of.

Both grannies had lived with him, Jane, and the girls as the girls were growing up, and it had been a very happy household. Ann and Mabel were both widows, so they had had plenty of time to devote to their granddaughters. They had each also been very willing babysitters whenever he or Jane had to leave the house. The girls adored them both - their two very loving, but very *different* grandmothers.

Mabel, Arthur's loud, outspoken mother, had been widowed when she was just 53 years old. His dad, Arthur senior, had died suddenly and without warning, keeling over on the docks one cold February morning while he was unloading bags of sugar. It was raw sugar sent from some distant, tropical land - apparently it should never have been unloaded that day as the chilly temperature outside threatened to ruin the product. However, an overzealous warehouse manager had decided to proceed with moving the bags against all advice. Tragedy ensued. While trying to manoeuvre the heavy jute bags, Arthur senior slipped on some black ice, instantly crushed by sweet stuff.

From that day on, Mabel refused to touch sugar. She would not cook with it, so there were no more delicious cakes or puddings for the family to enjoy. She would not even use it to sweeten her cup of tea, whereas, before the tragedy, she always enjoyed at least three heaped teaspoons full of it in her cup. From the day her husband died until the day *"I get lowered into the ground,"* she never intended to let another speck of sugar touch her lips.

Living life a little less sweetly was a hardship, but it was nothing compared to losing her husband, the man she had loved passionately since she was a young girl of sixteen. He was the father of her twelve children, most of whom died long before their time as well. At least, she thought, he would have their company when he got to heaven.

Sometimes, when she felt really maudlin, she wished she was in heaven already too, sitting on some beautiful cloud surrounded by her loving husband and the babies who never made it past infancy.

But of course, most of the time, she was glad to still be alive. If for nothing else, she was happy to get to spend time with her son, Arthur, his lovely wife Jane, and their beautiful girls - her granddaughters. And today was so special, the day their baby girl, Louisa, would marry a young man of whom they had all become rather fond, the young man of her dreams.

GRANNY ANN'S STORY

Ann Seed, now known as Granny Ann, was born in 1831 in North London. Her family, although not rich, was better off than most of their neighbours.

Her great-grandfather had come to England as a young man in the early 1700s, acting as the servant to a French Huguenot silk merchant. He settled with the family into a splendid house in Spitalfields. Over the years, Great-Grandfather had learnt the trade well, becoming one of the most successful weavers of his generation. His children and grandchildren followed in his footsteps, spending most of their lives sitting in dingy attic rooms making the most beautiful silk garments for the aristocracy. However, in the mid-1800s, cheaper fabrics like calico became fashionable, and the silk industry declined.

The once sought-after houses in Spitalfields became less desirable, and many of the old Huguenot families moved out of London to places like Sudbury, Braintree, and Colchester.

Ann's ancestors decided to stay in London; it was the only home they had ever known. By the time Ann was born, her parents were settled in Islington, in a little rented townhouse on a quiet street.

Ann's father still dabbled in silk, taking the odd commission for wealthy clients. Although he was known as one of the very best silk makers in London, he did not charge high prices; instead, he enjoyed seeing the pleasure his handiwork gave his customers. This drove his wife mad.

"For heaven's sake, why do you charge so little? They would all be happy to pay double - maybe even *three times* as much for your work. They know you are by far the best silk worker in London."

During times like this, he would just give her one of his quiet smiles and she would know she had lost. Her husband was such a kind, gentle man - a talented man who had no intention of overcharging for his services.

Young Ann would listen to these conversations between her parents, knowing that in some ways, they were both right. Her dad *did* charge too little for his work, but she understood why he did it. He felt that his was a God-given talent, not to be overcharged for at any price. He had never quite shaken off the long-held views of all his ancestors, views that went right back to when his grandfather first came to England with the Huguenots - all Protestants escaping religious persecution.

"By the way, my dears, I had a very interesting young man come into the showroom today." Ann, her mother, and her brother all sat up straight to listen. Her father's stories were always so fascinating; he was such a natural storyteller, always embellishing things to make them a little more interesting.

"A nice lad came over from the other side of the river - Southwark, I think he said. Anyway, he wanted to buy some of my silk, old, cut-off bits that he thought I might let him have for a cheap price."

"But why would he want old bits like that, Dad? What on earth could he do with them?"

Ann's brother, a rather pompous young man who had never had to struggle for anything in his life, asked the question in a lazy, rather bored way.

"Well, Son, not every lad is born into such comforts as you are. I admired him for his enterprise and sent him away with a box full of stuff. I told him the only price I wanted was to see what he managed to do with it."

Ann and her mother smiled. How generous he was.

"Well, I think that's silly. What on earth is a poor boy from the slums going to do with all that silk? You could have kept it, Dad, and made me a few new kerchiefs."

Ann often wondered why her brother was so selfish, so uncharitable, so unlike their loving father.

Two years after that conversation, Ann's father was dead, knocked over and killed by a horse and cart on Regent Street while he was delivering a box of silk waistcoats to a gentleman's outfitters. It had been pandemonium - horses bolting, women screaming, and blood dripping all over the box of beautiful waistcoats.

Ann and her mother were bereft.

He had been such a fine man - a good husband and wonderful father.

Ann's brother quickly took charge of the family.

He had no interest in the silk business other than taking the money that came from it to support his rather lavish lifestyle. He decided to shut it down, sacking all the workers without giving any notice or recompense. He sold the work-room premises; with the money he got, he continued to purchase fancy items, bed all the actresses and shopgirls he could manage, and gamble every night in backstreet dens.

Like most women of the era, Ann and her mother had to sit back and watch as he frittered their fortunes away. They had no rights to anything; according to the law, all decisions, money, and property went to the first-born son... even if he was totally unsuitable for such responsibilities.

Ann was just 26 years old when her father died and by her 27th birthday, everything they had was all gone. The rented house on the nice, quiet street, the silk workroom, most of their possessions, and all their money. Her wretched brother had spent the lot.

On the day the bailiffs came to remove them all from the house, her brother was missing. Absent, so he didn't have to face the consequences of his actions. Ann and her mother had stood there helplessly, as the door to their beloved home was boarded up and they had to walk away. They had three small trunks between them, which carried a few of their clothes and other small treasures.

For weeks, they stayed in a friend's spare room. This friend, once a trusted employee of Ann's father, felt desperately sorry for them both. However, he was poor himself, so they could not rely on his generosity for too long.

Over time, Ann saw her mother getting more and more desperate - losing her mind a little, day by day. She had never been a particularly strong or capable woman, and had been used to her late husband doing everything for her. In addition, she had to cope with the shame of knowing that her *son, her own dear boy*, had cheated her out of her home and future.

In the end, it became just too much for her to bear. She began to roam the streets, taking her clothes off and desperately offering her body to any passing man.

Ann would remember the day they came to cart her mother off to the Bedlam Asylum for the rest of her life.

Bedlam... The "madhouse," "a palace for lunatics." After some time, they changed the name to the Bethlem Royal Hospital. The new building was situated at St. George's Fields on Lambeth Road in Southwark, instead of in the splendid old building in the city at Bishopsgate. It may have been a new building - erected after the original Bedlam was torn down in 1815 - but it was still a place of dread, a place where lost souls were sent to die.

Ann absolutely hated visiting her mother there, but like the good, dutiful daughter she was, she tried to go most weeks - once a month at the very least. It made her desperately unhappy to see her mother in that dreadful place, watching her slowly decline over the months, then years. She saw her change from the once vibrant, rather spoilt woman she had been into a thin, wraith of a creature with dirty, uncombed hair and wild eyes. Ann was told, in no uncertain terms, that her mother would never be released - that she would have to spend the rest of her days in that dark, dismal place.

Ann's brother never once went to visit their mother, of course. Ann later heard that he had been chased out of town by a gang of East End criminals whom he had cheated at a card game. Apparently, to escape their wrath, he had run away to sea with one of his actress friends.

Thus, life was hard and lonely for Ann. She managed to find a job at a little factory, sewing bits of offcut leather onto hats, but it was hard, laborious work and she hated it. One day, her boss, a rather unpleasant little man who was always trying to back her into a dark corner of the factory and lift up her skirts, told her he needed a delivery done "*sharpish*" over the river. As their usual delivery man was already out for the day, he had decided Ann could do it instead.

"Earn yourself a bit extra this week, my dear. I'll give you the money for the omnibus to Southwark and enough left over for a nice cup of tea. There's plenty more there if you treat me right."

Ann fumed all the way to the bus stop. How dare he imply she would trade her favours for a bit of extra cash?

The parcel she was carrying was bulky and awkward. She tried to tuck it under her arm, but it was a bit too heavy. Inside were twenty tweed caps, all finished off with a bit of leather. Some had a big leather button sewn on the crown, others had their brims trimmed with soft leather in shades of brown, green, and black to match the tweed fabric. She was supposed to deliver them to the hat shop on Borough Road, near the market.

After getting off the bus, Ann walked along the cobbled streets carefully, balancing the heavy parcel in both hands and trying to avoid all the puddles that threatened to soak the hem of her coat. It was the only coat she possessed.

"I say, miss - would you like me to help you with that? It looks a bit too heavy for a pretty young lady like you."

Ann looked up at the speaker and found herself staring into the kindest brown eyes she had ever seen.

"Oh no, thank you so much, but really, I can manage. It isn't all that heavy actually; it's just a bit awkward."

"No, I insist," the man offered. "I notice from the label that it's going to Borough Hats. I'm going past that way myself, so it won't be any bother for me to carry it for you. You might get some feeling back in your arms in time to have a cup of tea with me afterwards, to say thank you!"

Ann laughed, despite knowing that she really shouldn't be talking to such a stranger - even if he was rather handsome and obviously very kind.

They walked along together in companionable silence for a while. At least now that her hands were free, she could hitch up her dress a little as they came to each puddle. Although she was careful to only raise it ever so slightly - so as not to expose too much ankle - she was acutely aware that he was studying her in a rather appreciative way. It had been a long time since she had attracted any male admirers (if you discounted her horrible boss with the wandering hands).

It surprised her how comfortable she felt with him.

While she dropped the parcel off at the menswear shop, he waited patiently outside. The elderly man who owned the shop opened each tissue-wrapped hat individually, checking each one over with a fine-tooth comb.

"Sorry my love, I know you're probably impatient to get back, but that old devil sometimes tries to cheat me with shoddy workmanship or a shortage of stock. This time though, it all looks very good. Be sure to tell him that whoever he's got sewing his hats these days is doing a splendid job. I know he's a mean old bugger, so here's half a crown to buy yourself a little something."

She came out of the shop feeling ten feet tall. Not only had he given her a tip of half a crown - a huge amount - but he had also praised the quality of her work. Of course, he hadn't realised that *she* was the one who had actually made the caps; after all, it was hardly considered women's work!

The young man, whose name was Albert Seed, had been lounging against the brick wall. He stood to attention as she came out of the shop.

"Okay, my darling, where are you planning to take me for this cuppa, then?"

In the end, they decided on the little café in Borough Market. It was busy there, a very public place, so no-one could accuse them of behaving inappropriately. It seemed as though he knew everyone.

"Morning, Albert. How's it going?"

"Hey Albert, nice day for it."

"Who's your lady friend, Albert? Ain't you going to introduce us?"

To all these questions, he merely smiled and said:

"Just enjoying a nice cuppa with my new lady friend. Not that it's any of your business."

"Hey Albert, why don't you take some of this nice cod home for your mum? You know she's partial to a nice bit of fish."

"Okay, Mabel. I'll come back when I've escorted this lady to her carriage."

While they were waiting for the bus to take Ann back over the river, back to the dreary factory and her even drearier digs, Albert spoke about himself, telling her that he came from a big family. He discussed how his father, grandfather, and all his brothers and uncles worked on the river as boatmen or dockers. He said he never wanted to do that; he had wanted to become a tailor or an artist instead, but had struggled to find an apprenticeship to do either.

"Then one day, a bloke I met in the pub was talking about all the old silk weavers, and how most of them had left London. He said that there were still a few small work-rooms around, so I started making enquiries. After roaming the streets for a few weeks, I heard about a bloke up Islington way, an old French bloke who ran a little workshop turning out quality silkwear for the big London shops. I called in on the off-chance. He was such a nice old chap, really interested in me and my big plans, and he sent me away with a box full of silk material. They were offcuts from all the jobs he'd done.

I was thrilled, reckoned they were worth a pretty packet. Next day, I went and saw one of the old Jewish tailors down near Borough Market and got him to show me how to make ties. Now, I've got a nice little business making silk ties.

I went back to Islington a few months later to show the old bloke what I'd done; he was so pleased he gave me another box of offcuts. In fact, he kept me going with supplies for the first year or two, but then he got killed - run over by a horse and cart on Regent Street. I was very sad when I heard that - he was such a nice old gent. Without his generosity, I would never have got to be where I am today... a world-class tie cutter."

Ann was stunned. What an incredible coincidence. She remembered that day so well, the day her father had given a poor lad a box of offcuts. How pleased he would have been if he were still alive, to see how well that young man had done.

After that, their friendship blossomed. To Ann, it seemed as though her father had sent Albert to her, a gift from heaven. He was good-looking, well-mannered, generous, and kind... exactly the kind of young man her father would have approved of.

She told her mother about Albert when she visited her next, but sadly, her mother was past caring. Past caring about herself, her daughter, or any young man she might have taken a liking to.

In all honesty, there was no reason for Ann *not* to pursue the friendship. She had nothing and no-body else in her life, especially no-body to raise objections to her friendship with a young man who came from a working-class family in a rough part of town. Albert was certainly not as genteel as the young men Ann would have been mixing with if she still lived on the quiet little street in leafy Islington, but somehow, he was perfect.

Ann grew to love Albert's large, noisy family, and they were so happy to see their boy in love that they welcomed her with open arms. In no time at all, she had given up her dreary digs and her job with the horrible boss, and had moved to Southwark, sharing a bedroom in the old tenement block with Albert's three sisters. He taught her how to make ties and was delighted when she picked it up in no time. She loved the feel of the silk between her fingers as she sewed. It reminded her of her father and other, happier times. It was a wonderful link to her past life.

Exactly a year to the day after they met, Ann and Albert became engaged; two months after that, they were married in the little parish church where Albert had been christened. Half of his huge family sat on the bride's side of the church and the other half sat on the groom's side, that way, no idle onlookers would realise that Ann had been all alone in the world, apart from her mother in the lunatic asylum and her runaway rotter of a brother.

Ann and Albert were ecstatically happy in their new life together. It was everything they had both dreamed of. Albert had a beautiful, gentle wife who adored him, and Ann had a loving, devoted husband who would give her the moon if she asked for it. They moved into their own room in the tenement block where he had grown up, and she quickly became part of his loving family.

When their baby girl, whom they decided to call Jane, arrived in 1861 - just a year after their wedding - the whole family rejoiced.

Sadly, there were no more babies after that. Ann had a couple of miscarriages - babies lost before they even made it into the world - and although they were devastated, at least living in such close proximity to their family ensured that there were always plenty of little ones to love and care for.

In the meantime, Jane flourished. She was a tiny little thing, much smaller than her cousins of the same age, but her lack of stature never held her back. She could hold her own against the biggest of them and was the best at having the last word in any discussion. Her little voice was often heard echoing around the concrete square between the huge tenement blocks.

"Come on, John, you *know* it's Maisie's turn with the rope. You had your go already; don't try and cheat."

"If you don't let go of her hair this instant, I'm going to run inside and tell your mum."

"Who wants some of this toffee? My mum made it yesterday!"

"Did you see that funeral down the high street yesterday? Bet that was some rich bloke, all those horses and flowers piled high."

"You should have seen the pile of ties my mum and dad made yesterday. I think we'll be millionaires by the time I'm eleven."

Jane was a bright and generous girl, loved by so many. She did well in school. Although she wasn't naturally gifted academically, she was very determined and so tried her very best. In fact, if you had to sum up Jane Seed at any time during her life, that is what you would have said: "She tried her very best."

When Jane was 16 years old, she caught the eye of Arthur Plant.

Arthur, another tenant of Peabody Buildings, lived just across the square. For years, he had admired the little curly-headed girl with the loud voice. He admired her pluck and the way she stood up to any bigger kids who tried to bully her or her friends. However, he had never looked at her as anything other than a little kid; after all, she was six years younger than him. Hardly "girlfriend material."

One day, that all changed. Arthur was just wandering back through the square after taking his weekly bath in the communal bathhouse. He noticed a few women were hanging out some washing, and slowed down as he passed.

"Hello, young Arthur. How's your dad doing? I was sorry to hear about his accident. They say he's lucky he didn't lose both legs."

"Oh, thanks, Mrs. B. I'll tell him you asked after him. Must dash now, promised my nephews I'd take them to the park for a look at the duck pond."

He was just about to walk away when a figure emerged from behind the big white sheets that had just been pegged up on the line.

For a moment he thought his heart had stopped. It felt like all the blood was draining from his body, although in reality, he knew he was blushing.

"Oh, hello. I don't think I've seen you 'round here before. Have you just moved in?"

He knew that the old ladies had noticed his blushes, and one of them spoke with a chuckle in her voice.

"For gawd's sake, Arthur, of course you know her! This is Jane, Albert and Ann Seed's little 'un. Not that she's so little now of course, are you Jane, love?"

Arthur smiled weakly and hurried away. How could that possibly be little Jane - the same girl who had chased him and his mates away after they tried to steal the little kids' apples that had been scrumped from the communal orchard and hidden in the old, wooden crate trolley? Or the small girl who shouted at the drunken man who stole the tatty old gloves off the Guy Fawkes she had made?

Arthur found himself thinking about Jane all weekend. He marched back and forth across the square, hoping to catch another glimpse of her.

It took two whole weeks before he spotted her again, this time at Borough Market, carrying a big, wicker basket of shopping and trailing behind her mother, who was stopping to chat at every stall. As they approached the fish stall, Arthur knew he had found his opportunity. His mum, Mabel, was serving behind the counter, so it would seem perfectly natural for him to be there, too.

"Good morning, Ann, love. What can I get you? Got some nice bits of cod and haddock today. Or some herring, sprats, or eels. Sold out of mussels and oysters already - bit of a run on those today - but should have plenty more tomorrow. What do you fancy, love? I know your Albert is always partial to a nice bit of fish and Jenny at the next stall has some lovely watercress that would go down a treat with it!"

"Oh, hello, Jane. How are you, love? My, you are turning into a pretty young lady! I expect the boys will all be sniffing around you soon; just make sure you save yourself for someone decent - a good man who really deserves you and will look after you well."

Presumably, both Jane and her parents thought that young Arthur was suitable - *a decent young man,* because just one week after that meeting in the fish market, he came to their flat and asked to see Albert, to get his permission to take Jane to the music hall the following Saturday.

After six months, it was obvious to everyone on the estate that the young couple was madly in love. The two became inseparable, always together, always smiling. They even held hands - when there was no one else around.

Arthur was desperate to marry Jane, to snap her up before any other, wealthier, more suitable suitors appeared. But Jane was still only 16 years old, hardly out of school, and her parents were not ready to let her go.

"Okay, my lad. If you treat her right, stay loyal, and keep her happy, you can ask me again in a year's time. Perhaps then, if she wants to, I will give you my permission to marry her."

Exactly one year to the day later, Arthur again approached his prospective father-in-law and this time, was ecstatic to receive his approval. He rushed straight down to the jeweller in Vauxhall High Street and picked out the biggest, shiniest ring he could afford.

That night, the whole of Peabody Buildings joined in the engagement celebrations. They had all watched the romance as it blossomed and were delighted for the young couple.

Six months later, on a sunny June day in 1879, everyone gathered in the square again to celebrate the wedding. Colourful homemade bunting was strung from one building to another and small children ran in and out of the open doors to the flats, screaming excitedly. Old tables had been borrowed from the market and were set up outside, covered in old white sheets as tablecloths. The sheets were necessary to hide the battered, old tabletops, which were mostly made from crates from the docks or bits of old furniture. Almost all of the tables were riddled with woodworm and years of overuse. Everyone had brought their own chairs, so it was a real mishmash. Someone had even brought some chairs over from the church hall. After all, the vicar was at the party; why not borrow some of his chairs?

The wedding ceremony had been marvellous. The little stone church was packed to the brim with family, friends, and well-wishers. Albert and Ann sat right at the front, watching proudly as their girl married the man of her dreams. Albert didn't mind admitting later (after a couple of pints of beer at the reception) that he had shed a couple of tears as he walked his girl down the aisle. "She looked just like her mum in that wedding dress, and it reminded me of our special day."

Ann had beamed across at him as he said this. Sometimes, she just couldn't believe her luck. Once upon a time, she had been a sad, lonely young woman with a sick mother in the asylum and no-one else in the world to turn to. Now look at her... she had a huge, noisy family surrounding her and her beloved daughter was following in her footsteps, marrying a good man who would look after her.

On the other side of the aisle, the groom's parents - Arthur senior and Mabel - were thrilled too. They were thrilled that their son was so happy. Since meeting Jane, Albert was a changed lad. He was more responsible and gave thought to the future rather than just going out to get drunk with his mates every Friday night. While not a saint - their boy would never be boring - that girl was certainly bringing out the best in him.

Arthur Plant and Jane Seed were married in 1879. Their first child arrived the following year.

Ann Plant, their first daughter, was born in 1880, and was followed two years later in 1882 by her sister, Amber. Little Astrid - later known as Tidy - appeared in 1884, and was followed exactly two years later by Alice, then Amy in 1888. Finally, their final girl, Louisa, affectionately known as Lou, graced the world with her presence in 1890.

Arthur never quite recovered. He went from being a carefree single man with hardly a worry in the world to becoming a husband and father to six beautiful daughters in the short space of just eleven years. It was an enormous amount of worry and responsibility, but he wouldn't change it for the world.

THE SIX PLANT GIRLS

Arthur and Jane had never imagined that they would end up as the parents of six children, let alone six girls! When they had idly daydreamed - as all young, engaged couples do - about the kind of family they would have, they both imagined themselves with perhaps two children. Ideally they would have a son first, then a little daughter. That would be the perfect-sized family - big enough, but not *too* big.

When little Ann, their firstborn, arrived just a year after their wedding day, they were ecstatic. She was healthy and beautiful and Jane, being such a young mother, had no trouble delivering her. She was born at home in Peabody Buildings, in her parents' bed, with the old midwife and several women family members in attendance. The two grandmothers-to-be, Mabel and Ann, were hovering by the bed the whole time, nagging the other women to fetch hot water and clean towels.

Little Ann was just toddling when her sister Amber arrived two years later. She too was born in the same bedroom - in the same bed - with both grannies and several aunties in attendance. Arthur was hovering outside the room, waiting for the midwife to come out and tell him he was the proud father of a boy, so it came as rather a surprise to hear it was another girl. He really didn't care, though, as long as his babies and their mother were well and happy. That was good enough for him.

But Jane knew how disappointed he was, even though he tried so hard to hide it. That is why exactly two years later, in 1884, she was in labour again, desperate to produce a son for her beloved husband.

Baby Astrid, later known as Tidy, arrived in a very quiet, easy way, and of course, her besotted father welcomed his third daughter with open arms.

"Jane, my darling. I've just realised that you're giving all our girls names that begin with 'A.' Why is that? I don't mind, of course, I love the names you've chosen. But I wonder if there is a reason, or if it is just a coincidence?"

Jane was sitting up in bed, nursing the latest baby while the other two girls ran around the room squealing excitedly, delighted that they had a new sister.

"Oh, Arthur, are you sure you don't mind? You know we named little Ann after my mum. It made her so happy, do you remember how she couldn't stop smiling for days? Then, I just fancied the name 'Amber'; it seemed so exotic. And as for this little one, well, somehow 'Astrid' just seems to suit her, don't you think? I promise if we have a boy, you can choose his name."

But that boy never materialised. When the next little girl was born in 1886, they named her Alice, then Amy joined the family in 1888.

Arthur was rather hoping five would be the end. He had long ago given up any hope of fathering a son, and to be honest, he really didn't care anymore. He just loved his young wife and their daughters with a passion, and would do anything in the world for each one of them.

When Jane was 29, she gave birth to their last child. By now, she had run out of names beginning with 'A,' so the new baby was named Louisa.

All the girls thrived. Arthur worked hard to make sure they could always pay the rent on time and put enough food on the table to feed the girls. When they weren't at school or sitting at the old pine kitchen table eating the delicious meals their mother had prepared, they were outside, in the square, playing with their cousins and all the other kids from the buildings. It was a very happy childhood for them all.

On Sundays - Arthur's only day off - they would all dress in their Sunday best and go to church. Then, they would go home for a big roast lunch, although sometimes they had fish rather than meat, as it was cheaper.

On Sunday nights, they would all have a bath. Jane would boil kettles of water on the range and Arthur would fill the old tin bath. Sitting in the bath, two at a time in front of the roaring coal fire, the girls would laugh as their parents waltzed around the little kitchen or as their father told them funny stories about people he had met at the market. It was a very happy household, a household filled with love and laughter.

A household that expanded when both Arthur and Jane's mothers were widowed at a young age.

Arthur's father was killed in the sugar accident at the docks when Mabel was just fifty-three years old. Jane's mother, Ann, lost her beloved Albert a year later, when he dropped dead of a heart attack one day. He had been in the middle of completing an order of silk ties for a big department store in Oxford Street, and despite her grief, Ann insisted on finishing and delivering all of them to the store herself.

"I'm not having anyone think my Albert wasn't a man of his word. He promised them those ties, so I'm going to make sure I don't let him down."

She worked day and night to fulfill her promise, and when she delivered them to the store, the menswear department manager was shocked at her appearance. A bereft widow in her mourning clothes - the black of the attire matching the dark circles under her eyes. Her eyes were worn out from weeping. The manager admired her bravery and offered her more work, but she sadly declined.

"I'm so sorry, sir, but without my Albert, my heart just isn't in it anymore. I won't be making any more ties."

And she never did. Instead, she devoted herself to her daughter, son–in–law, and six granddaughters.

Arthur, being such an honourable man, could not bear to see his widowed mother or mother-in-law struggling to look after themselves and being at the mercy of other people. So, he had insisted they both come to live with him, Jane, and the girls.

The Plant girls, his fabulous, feisty daughters. All so different and yet such a united force. If one of them was upset, they were all upset. If one was happy, they were all happy. In fact, they were all happy almost all of the time. After all, they had a roof over their heads, two loving parents, plenty of food to fill their stomachs, and clean clothes to wear. Of course, most of these clothes were second hand, originally hand-me-downs from a bigger cousin which were then passed down to each younger sister in turn as the older ones outgrew them.

Ann was the lucky one, of course. As the eldest, she got to wear everything first. But it didn't take long at all before she outgrew them; by the age of twelve she was almost as tall as her father, already a good few inches taller than her mother.

Amber got the garments next, but she grew quickly too, so they were soon passed down to Astrid. The three youngest sisters, Alice, Amy, and Louisa, watched as the coveted dresses became a little more faded, a little shabbier, and yet they still couldn't wait to inherit them.

All the girls grew to be taller than both their parents, except for little Louisa. Like her mum, Lou was short, only just reaching five feet tall if she stood up really straight. But truthfully, she didn't care. Her dad always hugged her when her sisters teased her about being "*such a little tich,*" and he would explain to the weeping little girl that "*all the best things come in small packages. Don't listen to those sisters of yours. Your mum is only small too, and she's the most magnificent woman in the world - even better than the old Queen was.*"

Louisa had seen plenty of pictures of old Queen Victoria and knew that she, too, had been quite tiny. In fact, she had even seen her in person once. She remembered going to watch the Queen's Diamond Jubilee procession back in 1897, when she was just seven years old. It had been such an exciting day; it seemed like the whole of London was there to see *their* Queen.

The Plants had been hoping to stand on London Bridge to get a really good view of the procession, but when they got there it had been closed off to the public. Instead, it was lined with troops, all smartly dressed in their uniforms, standing to attention on either side of the bridge and waiting to salute as the Queen passed.

So, Louisa, her sisters, and most of the population of Southwark - all dressed in their Sunday best - stood with the crowds, shoulder to shoulder, cheering wildly as the procession passed them. It was a marvellous sight: the colours, the spectacle, the excitement. The sheer pageantry of it all was overwhelming. There were so many grand carriages in the procession and as each one arrived, little Louisa peered into them, sure that *this one* must definitely be the Queen's carriage. She was sitting up high on her dad's shoulders, and every time she got excited, Arthur would groan. "Blimey, Lou, you may be just a little scrap of a thing, but you sure are heavy. I reckon you must weigh at least a ton!"

Her sisters were all standing in front, right by the bridge, to get a bird's eye view. It was lucky they were all tall enough to see without having to be balanced on someone's shoulders like little Louisa.

Suddenly, the crowd went quiet, and a sense of anticipation rippled through the waiting crowd.

"Here she comes. Here comes our Queen."

The band started playing and everyone stood to attention. The men all took off their hats as the carriage approached them. It was a splendid thing - an open landau pulled by a team of magnificent horses. The horses were weighed down by highly-decorated harnesses and shining brasses. Little Louisa had never seen such a magnificent sight.

Spontaneously, the crowd burst into song: "*God save our gracious queen. Long live our noble queen.*"

"Oh, Dad, she's so tiny."

A few people standing near them smiled at the little girl's words.

Arthur smiled back at them. His girl was right. The old Queen was tiny, in fact, she almost looked like a little doll sitting in the huge state carriage, a parasol shielding her from the sun.

Nonetheless, she was certainly magnificent, even after sixty years on the throne and losing her beloved husband, Prince Albert.

Everyone watched in awe as the carriage progressed. Queen Victoria smiled graciously to her subjects as she passed by them. To little Louisa and her sisters, it seemed as though her regal smile was intended just for them.

Sadly, the old Queen passed away just four years later, in 1901, and the whole country mourned. Her son, Edward VII, succeeded her, but he was never to be held in quite such esteem by his subjects as his old mother had been.

PEABODY BUILDINGS,
SOUTHWARK
1905

"**D**on't you think it's a bit funny that Mum used to be a 'Seed,' and now she's a 'Plant'?"

The four youngest Plant girls were sitting in the sunshine, in the middle of the concrete square outside their home.

"Yes, I guess that means their marriage was preordained."

"What does 'preordained' mean?"

Astrid, the third-born Plant girl and the eldest of this little group, pulled herself up to her full five feet, ten inch height.

At just 20 years old, there was still a chance she might grow a little bit more. It was her ambition to be taller than her two elder sisters, who were both almost six feet.

Six feet - so tall for young ladies. They were unusual, the Plant girls, known throughout the borough for their height and good looks. It was undeniable that all six of Arthur's daughters were very pretty, just like their mother.

Astrid smiled to herself as she thought about her sisters, Ann and Amber, both so grown up now at 24 and 22, respectively. In fact, they were so grown up that Amber was about to have a baby any minute. That's why the younger ones had all been shooed out of the house; the old midwife had just arrived. It probably wouldn't be long now before they heard a baby wailing.

Astrid had no intention of ever having a baby herself. Instead, she was going to be a famous novelist.

"'Preordained' means something that was already planned out, meant to be. Something that God decided should happen."

In truth, Astrid wasn't exactly sure what "preordained" meant. She had read the word in a novel she picked up at the penny library, but knew there was no point asking her mum, dad, *or* elder sisters what it meant. None of them were readers like she was. She would much rather curl up in front of the fire, in one of the old kitchen chairs while reading a book, than go shopping, walking, or even out socialising like her big sisters. She was much happier losing herself in a good novel; she thought it better to read about the lives and trials of other young women than to actually have to live them herself. The mere thought of having a boy pay attention to her was more than she could stand. Leave *that* to her silly sisters. Look where it gets you to be involved with men, anyway - writhing around on a bed in agony, trying to give birth to a baby who will just take over your life for the next twenty years! No thanks. Motherhood was not her cup of tea - her sisters were welcome to it all.

"Astrid, you haven't answered my question. Don't you think it's funny that Mum was called 'Jane Seed,' then when she married Dad, she became 'Jane Plant'? Such a coincidence that the two names match. Imagine if she'd married a Mr. Tray. Seed, Tray, do you get it?"

Astrid rolled her eyes as her sisters laughed. They were so juvenile sometimes.

Still, one day, she planned to move out - away from Peabody Buildings and Southwark. She longed to go north of the river, to rent a little garret somewhere up West. Maybe she'd live in the attic rooms of a famous author who would encourage her to use her God-given talents to write novels that the penny library - or even some big publishing house - would fight and clamour over.

That was another word she had read in the latest book: "clamour."

She really wished she could join the new public library on Borough Road. She loved walking past the splendid old building and often hung around on the steps there, just watching the people going in and out.

The people she watched on the steps were lucky people, rich enough to afford the guarantee fee of ten shillings. Most people she knew in Southwark only earned about twice that much in a whole year. Maybe one day, lending libraries would become available to everyone. For now though - in this year of 1905 - as far as she could see, they were only for the rich. They were not yet meant for poor people like her to enjoy.

Of course, if she ever *were* fortunate enough to join, she would make sure she never kept any books longer than allowed; there was no way she could afford to pay the extortionate overdue fines of a penny a week!

Lost in thought, dreaming of a splendid future surrounded by mountains of books as far as the eye could see, Astrid was rudely awakened by the squalling cry of a new baby.

"Oh, sounds like our Amber's done it. Hope it's a boy; Dad would be so happy to have another man around."

All six of the Plant girls were very aware that, although their Dad never alluded to it, in his heart he would have loved a son. So, a grandson would be a good second best.

After another half hour, the old midwife came shuffling across the square.

"Hello, my little loves. Looks like you've got another girl in the family. She and your sister are doing just fine. I expect you'll be allowed in to meet the little one soon. If she grows up to be half as lovely as you lot, she'll do well. Seems like no time at all since I delivered all of you, especially you, young Lou. You've all grown into such good girls, a real credit to your mum and dad."

ANOTHER GENERATION
OF PLANT GIRLS

The new baby was christened Felicity.

When her sisters queried the baby's name, Amber, who was sitting up in bed nursing her new little red-headed infant, answered with a chuckle.

"Well, I expect lots of folks 'round here will think it's a bit too posh for a baby from the Buildings, but we've got big plans for this little one. My Fred reckons she's going to be a doctor or a lawyer. I don't really care about none of that, as long as she grows up happy and healthy, but my Fred's got big ideas. He doesn't want us spending our whole lives here in Southwark; he wants to spread our wings a bit - maybe go down south to the seaside. He says the air is much fresher down there and that it will be much better for this little one. Mind you, the midwife says I won't be going no-where for the next couple of weeks. She says I've got to stay right here in this bed, otherwise my milk will dry up and this little one will starve."

Her five sisters listened as they crowded around the bed to get a better view of their new baby niece. After that remark, they gave each other a knowing grin. Their Amber had always been so dramatic!

At this rate, she would never get 'round to having the half-dozen babies she always said she wanted, if she was going to spend a whole fortnight in bed each time she gave birth. Most of the women on the square were back on their feet after a couple of days, looking after their other kids and even pegging out their own washing. Heaven knows what they would think if they could hear Amber going on now.

But of course, Amber now had her Fred. Fred, the wide boy.

None of them were quite sure exactly how he made his money, but he certainly made plenty of it. At least he wasn't mean, thank goodness. The little bedroom they were all standing in now was chock a block full of things he had bought for the baby. There was a white wooden cot, a high chair, and a big, upright pram, just like the ones the upper classes had for their babies. On a chair were piles of new baby clothes, little tiny vests, cotton dresses, and hand-knitted cardigans, bonnets, and mittens.

"Blimey, Amber, you've got enough stuff here to clothe three babies, maybe even four."

"I know, Alice. But my Fred says he doesn't want me or little Felicity to want for nothing. He says we are to have the very best that London can offer. I do feel a bit embarrassed that I've got so much when some of the other young mothers in the square can't even afford to buy *one* set of new clothes for their baby."

Astrid snorted and turned away from the bed in disgust.

In her view, their Amber had always been a bit precocious and had always wanted more than their parents could afford to provide. Since marrying this Fred bloke, she seemed to have got worse, seemed to have turned into a real snob. If she really felt bad about having so much, she would be offering some of that big pile of baby clothes to the other young mothers in the Buildings, not just keeping it all for herself.

"Where does he get all the money to buy this stuff from anyway, Amber? He never seems to go out and do any hard work - not like Dad does."

Ann spoke sharply. As the eldest, she sometimes felt that it fell on her to ask all the hard questions and make sure that the girls all behaved themselves.

"Oh, for goodness sake, Ann, stop being so jealous just because your John can't give you the same luxuries. I thought you'd all be happy for me, but I can see you're not. I think it's time you all went home now. Me and Felicity need a snooze, and if I get too worked up my milk won't come properly. Then you'll all be responsible for making your little niece starve to death!"

Of course, little Felicity didn't die of starvation. In fact, she thrived. Amber and Fred treated her like a little doll, dressing her in long, frilly dresses with matching pantaloons underneath. There was always a new bonnet on her little head, and even before she could walk, her indulgent parents had bought her several pairs of small, leather button boots.

The other young mothers on the square looked long-ingly at the splendid sight and then back to their little ones, who were sitting quietly in their tatty, old prams wearing second-hand rags. These poor children often had holes in their shoes or no shoes at all, and it seemed rather unfair.

After all, that toffee-nosed Amber Plant was no better than any of them. The only difference was that all the money her Fred earned came from questionable sources, whereas they knew how hard their own husbands worked - doing back-breaking work at the docks or the market for a few measly shillings just to feed their families.

By the time Lou and Eustace got married, Amber had two children - two girls - both happy, healthy, and rather spoilt. Fred had done exactly as he promised: whisked them all away from Southwark, away from Peabody Buildings, and away from the bosom of their family. The four of them moved to live in a little semi-detached house on the seafront in Eastbourne.

As the eldest of the six sisters, Ann Plant had no intention of ever leaving Southwark. She loved every street, every grimy alleyway. She loved walking along to Borough Market and being recognised by so many people. Generations of her dad's family had lived in the area, going back decades. Her Granny Mabel even sat the girls down often to tell them bits of the family history.

Ann was fascinated by it all. Other people like her sisters, especially Amber and Astrid, might have had ambitions to move away, to make a different kind of life. However, Ann was perfectly content. She had been born in Peabody Buildings, had married her childhood sweetheart, John, and lived in a flat on the block opposite her mum and dad. To add to her joy, she had given birth to a beautiful baby boy. She had been so proud to be the first one to give her dad a grandson.

She would never forget the tears that ran freely down her beloved father's face when he first set eyes on little Arthur. Of course she had named her baby after him! After all, he was going to be the most important granddad in the world.

There hadn't been any more babies for her after Arthur. Something to do with "women's troubles," the old doctor at the hospital had said. But after the initial disappointment, she found she didn't really mind at all. Her little boy was an absolute joy - the sweetest, smartest, cleverest little one who ever lived. And of course, he was her dad's little shadow. Wherever Arthur senior went, little Arthur was sure to follow. They walked the streets together, fed the ducks, wandered 'round the market chatting to all the stallholders, and sometimes, ventured down to the docks so that the little boy could see all the boats. Granddad Arthur showed little Arthur the big ships carrying their cargo, the little fishing boats, and the passenger boats, ferrying their customers from one side of the river to the other.

"Granddad, is it true that everybody - our whole entire family - has always worked on the river? Aunty Alice says not one person has ever worked anywhere else. She says that none of them have any idea how to live more than six feet from the river or the market. Is that true?"

Little Arthur spent all his time listening to the adults around him, which in some ways made him a rather precocious little boy. But he had a sweet nature, like his mum, so people forgave him if he was occasionally a little too big for his boots.

Arthur bent down and gave the little boy a hug.

"Oh yes, my lad, that's very true. All of us Plants have been in Southwark forever. Although of course, your Great-Granny Ann came from up North, the land across the river. But she's been here a long time now, so she's one of us."

The little boy stood at the Southward end of London Bridge and stared across the vast expanse of water. He just couldn't imagine anyone choosing to live over on the other side, especially his quiet little great-granny.

His Aunty Astrid had told him lots of stories about the kind of people who lived over there: artists, writers, and all the rich folk, like the king and queen. She said there were poor people too, who lived in the slums of the East End. Little Arthur knew that was right, because sometimes his uncles went over there to the music hall and came back moaning about all the dark alleyways, the pickpockets, and the orphans sleeping rough in the streets.

He had even seen it for himself once, when his mum and dad took him for an adventure. Well, he hadn't actually seen it *all*; he never saw a pickpocket or a dark alleyway, as it was daylight when they went. They had left home really early, about seven o'clock in the morning, and walked all the way across London Bridge. Then, they walked for miles past lots of big buildings, including the Tower of London, St. Paul's Cathedral, and Buckingham Palace, where the King lived. He had been a bit disappointed not to see any royalty, but he had really enjoyed watching all the soldiers in their smart red uniforms and big bearskin hats march back and forth across the palace grounds.

He got a bit tired after that, so his dad hoisted him up to give him a piggyback ride. That was even better; from up there, he could see so much more.

They had stopped at Lyons Corner House for a cup of tea and a sticky bun. He had rather hoped they might have lunch there, but his mum said it was too expensive. Anyway, she'd packed a flask and some bloater sandwiches so they could have those sitting on the grass in the park. It had been a lovely day, but little Arthur had been glad when they got back over the river, back to their own side.

"Granddad?"

"Yes, lad."

"Do you think the people on the other side are nice?"

"What do you mean, 'nice'?"

"You know, are they kind, or do they beat people up and make all the kids starve?"

Arthur senior tried not to laugh.

"Oh, lad. Whoever told you that rubbish? The people on the North Side are just the same as us. A few are maybe not so nice, but you get that wherever you live. Most folk are just downright decent, like we are."

The little boy put his small hand into his grandfather's big, weathered one, and continued chatting as they walked.

"Aunty Amber says that anyone who stays stuck in Southwark must need their head tested. What does that mean, Grandad?"

Arthur made a mental note to talk to all his daughters when he got home. How dare they fill this little lad's head with such rubbish?

"I think the ones who need their heads tested are your Aunty Amber and Aunty Astrid."

The way he said it made the little boy laugh, and they continued their walk along the River Thames in companionable silence for a while.

"Granddad, you know Aunty Lou is getting married on Saturday? Mum says I have to wear my Sunday suit, but I don't like it much. It's a bit scratchy."

"I know just what you mean, lad. I don't like wearing my suit much either, but your Gran will have our guts for garters if we turn up at the church wearing our comfortable old clothes."

BACK TO THE WEDDING DAY

Lou's wedding day started out warm and sunny.

It was sunny in every meaning of the word, which was very unusual for that time of the year. A good omen, Granny Ann said.

"Blooming remarkable, considering it's December and supposed to be the coldest day of the year. We all thought Lou was mad to get married on Christmas Eve, but maybe we were wrong. Looks like there is no chance of a white Christmas though; the kids will be disappointed. They always look forward to making a few snowballs on Christmas Day."

Granny Mabel spoke in her usual forthright fashion and no-one, especially on today of all days, had any intention of correcting her - of reminding her that they hadn't had a white Christmas for the last three years.

Everyone turned up wearing their Sunday best. The groom was handsome and the beautiful bride arrived eventually, turning up just half an hour late on the arm of her proud father.

Two of the younger Plant sisters, Alice and Amy, walked behind Lou, wearing pale pink dresses and carrying little bunches of daffodils tied up with pink ribbon. Little Felicity was in the procession, too, but her dress was somewhat grander, a frothy concoction of pink satin and lace. Her devoted father had apparently sourced it *"down Finchley way."* Her younger sister was wearing a very similar one, but with slightly less lace. Felicity was definitely her father's favourite. Little Arthur looked smart in his Sunday suit, although he kept fiddling with the collar of his shirt, wishing he was wearing his old jersey with the holes instead.

The little church was packed; there were even people standing at the back and outside the church in the graveyard.

"Dearly beloved, we are here today to celebrate the marriage of Louisa and Eustace..."

As the newly-married couple came out of the church, it began to snow. Just little flakes, but enough to leave a white residue on the grass.

"Come on you lot, let's get these photographs taken quickly so we can all get off to the pub for the party. We'll freeze if we hang around here too long."

It seemed that Granny Mabel had forgotten her earlier remark about white Christmases. Now she was just desperate to get to the pub and have a few glasses of stout, or maybe even one of those fancy sherries... after all, it wasn't every day you got the last of your granddaughters married off.

Lou and Eustace had decided not to hold their wedding party in the Peabody Buildings square, where big celebrations usually took place. It was Christmas Eve, after all, so everyone wanted to get things ready for the next day when all the families would get together for a big roast dinner and maybe even to exchange a few presents. Certainly no-one would want to sit around outside in the cold, especially now that it was starting to snow. Instead they were all going to the Bulls Head, down by the docks.

It was a big public house, big enough to hold all the dockers, sailors, and working men who frequented it every Friday night after they got paid. But better still, there was a huge room upstairs, plenty big enough for a good old cockney knees up. Because the Plant family was so well known in the district and most of the menfolk were regulars at the Bulls Head, the landlord had let them have the room really cheaply. After all, he knew they would drink plenty of his ale, and his missus had stayed up all night cooking food for the wedding breakfast. His sister had made the wedding cake, a three-tier thing with big flower decorations on the top and trailing down the side. Even he had to admit that it was a fine bit of work - no doubt the lovely bride would be ecstatic when she saw it.

Of course Lou was thrilled when she saw the cake; it just added another bit of magic to her special day. The whole event had been so wonderful. Everyone - even her two old grannies - got a bit tipsy, intoxicated by the sheer excitement of it all.

She was now, at the grand old age of 23, married to the man of her dreams, her Eustace.

She had loved him since she was sixteen years old, since she had seen him standing on the corner of Southwark Street with all his mates. Lurking there, propped up by the lamppost, hoping to catch a glimpse of ladies' ankles as they hitched up their long dresses when they crossed the road. They had to do that to stop their dresses from getting spoilt by the big wet puddles, or worse, risk getting the horse muck that the carriage drivers hadn't bothered to clear up all over their hems.

She had been on her way home from work the first time she saw him. Her shift at the leather factory finished at five o'clock and by that time she was always pretty exhausted, having been on her feet since seven-thirty in the morning. It was hard work and pretty monotonous at times, but she loved it. She loved the camaraderie of the place. She knew most of the women who worked there - had known them all her life - so in a way, it was just like an extension of home... Except that she earnt money! Though not much, admittedly. Not as much as she could earn if she were a nanny or a nurse, like her mum and dad wanted her to be. But at the end of the week, she had enough to satisfy her needs. As long as she could buy a new dress every six months and maybe a new pair of button boots and a bonnet to match, that was good enough for her. Her two sisters, Alice and Amy, who were two and four years her senior, had both decided to go into service in a big mansion up Hampstead way. Despite their cajoling, that had never much appealed to Lou; she wanted her independence, not to have to kowtow to some rich old woman who treated her like a piece of old rubbish.

Surprisingly, her three elder sisters: Ann, Amber, and Astrid had all supported her decision. She wasn't like the other two girls. Where they were both soft-spoken and mild mannered, Lou didn't take kindly to being told what to do.

"Look, Alice, I know you and Amy are happy in service; you like your uniforms and everything, but I just couldn't do it. I couldn't bear some toffee-nosed old bloke telling me to polish his shoes, or worse, have to stop him from trying to get into my undergarments."

There was a stunned silence in the kitchen, then everyone laughed.

"Oh gawd, Lou, you wouldn't last five minutes at our place. You'd be out on your ear before you'd hardly set foot in the house. They wouldn't stand all your nonsense like we've had to put up with all these years."

Lou had been just fourteen when they had this conversation, and two months later she found herself a job at the old leather factory down by the docks. The factory was run in a dilapidated old warehouse, formerly used for storing raw cotton that had come from America and the West Indies.

The owner was a very grumpy old man. He had inherited the business from his father, but would have much preferred to be an innkeeper. He was very fond of the demon drink and would stagger back into the factory every afternoon, reeking of the stuff, having spent two hours in the bar of the Bulls Head. Then he would make a beeline for the youngest, prettiest girls, who had to sit at their machines while he lurched over them, breathing alcohol fumes.

"Blimey, Lou, you had a lucky escape today! I thought the old man was going to drag you into his office and have his wicked way with you. You got him so riled up."

As usual, he had come back from the pub inebriated and had gone straight for the youngest girl on the factory floor. Her name was Eunice. She was a tiny, timid little thing and came from one of the poorest, roughest families in Southwark. Her brothers were always in and out of prison, her granny was in Bedlam, and her mum and aunties plied their wares down at the docks. But Eunice, quiet as she was, wanted a better life for herself. She wanted to escape from all the squalor, crime, and shame she had grown up with. Working at the leather factory was a start - at least she earnt some money of her own - and who knows? In a few years she might have saved enough to follow her dreams.

"Just leave her alone. Can't you see she doesn't like it?"

Lou's voice rang out across the factory.

"Who said that? Louisa Plant, who the *hell* do you think you are? Do you want me to give you your cards right now? I can easily find some other soppy little girl to take your place, and she'd probably work a darn sight harder - not waste all her time gossiping like you lot do."

For a moment, sixteen-year-old Lou wished she hadn't said anything, wished she hadn't opened her big mouth. But she couldn't bear to see the way he bullied the young ones, picking on those like Eunice who were just doing their best to survive.

Anyway, her little comment had worked. The boss huffed and puffed, muttering under his breath about "ungrateful little urchins" but had left Eunice alone and marched up the old metal staircase toward his office. His office - the room with a huge glass window overlooking the factory floor so he could keep an eye on them all.

"Huh, I'd like him to have tried to have his wicked way with me. He wouldn't know what hit him. I'm saving myself for my husband, not some little old creep like him."

It was later that very afternoon when she spotted her future husband, Eustace, for the first time. There was just something about him, something different from all the other lads on the corner. His blue eyes had a real twinkle in them, and he tipped his hat as she passed - almost like she was a real lady, not just some factory girl.

She bumped into him again a few weeks later, and this time she let him walk alongside her. She was very impressed that he insisted on walking on the road side of the pavement.

"Well, Miss Louisa, a gent should always do that. To stop a lady getting splashed by a big puddle if a carriage goes too fast, or if there is ever a runaway horse or a ruffian who might hurt her.

Lou was very happy that he had such good manners.

Of course he was poor like her, just an ordinary chap. It turned out he lived just around the corner - still in Peabody Buildings, but in another block. His family members were all dockers and seamen. Just like hers, generations of his family had worked on the River Thames and had been christened, married, and buried in the old church. She knew from the very first day she saw him that she wanted to marry him, to be his wife, to have his children.

But they were young. Eustace was only a year older than Lou and had yet to sow his wild oats. He had big plans to run away to sea, to become a merchant sailor. He was nowhere near ready to take on a wife and children.

They walked out together a few times. It wasn't a proper courtship, but they both knew they had strong feelings for each other. Lou was inexperienced; she had only had a couple of mild crushes before. In the past, she had had crushes on boys who were way out of her reach, but this was different. Eustace was the same as most of the boys around the Buildings: a bit cocky and outspoken. And yet, she sensed there was something different about him, something that she found very attractive.

Eustace was not tall - he was nowhere near as tall as his older brothers - but he had a confident swagger. His lack of height was made up for by his good looks, charm, and excellent manners. His family had always teased him, saying he was "*obviously born on the wrong side of the blanket, not one of them at all.*"

When he was young, he had not really understood what they meant by this. He just thought that maybe because he was born in the summertime, when the heat in the Buildings was stifling due to a lack of windows and rather poor ventilation, that there had been no blankets on the bed. Maybe that was what his family meant by the "wrong side of the blanket."

As he got older, into his late teens, and learnt a bit more about the world, he realised that "wrong side of the blanket" meant you were illegitimate, born out of wedlock, perhaps the result of an illicit affair. He had been mortified. His mum and dad seemed so happy. He couldn't imagine his mum straying, having an affair with someone else. His dad worshipped the very ground she walked on.

Although he was shorter than his brothers, there was definitely a family likeness. He had the same twinkly blue eyes and the same shaped nose as his brothers. It was surely only his height, or lack thereof, that set him apart.

"Jim?"

His older brother had been christened "James," but they all called him Jim.

"Yes, Eustace?"

"You know how you lot always say I was born on the wrong side of the blanket? Don't you think that's a bit disrespectful to Mum?"

"What do you mean?"

"Well, you know. It kind of implies that she hasn't always been very loyal to Dad."

Jim, a very handsome man in his late twenties, tossed back his head and laughed."

"Oh my gawd, Eustace. How long have you been worrying about this?" "Mum, come and listen to this."

Their mother had just walked into the kitchen, carrying a basket of shopping from the market. She was a very attractive woman in her early fifties.

"Our Eustace thinks you cheated on Dad and that he isn't one of us."

She could see that her youngest son looked a bit tearful. This surprised her, because of all her sons, Eustace seemed to be the most confident, the cockiest one of them all.

"Oh lad, where on earth did you get that idea?"

She dumped her basket on the old pine kitchen table, walked over to her son, and enfolded him in her big strong arms. She felt him sink into her embrace, just like he had done when he was a little boy.

"It's 'cos you always talk about me being different, shorter, being born on the 'wrong side of the blanket.'" His voice trailed off as he spoke.

"Oh lad, how long have you been carrying this worry around with you?"

She was a proud Cockney. A woman who had had to work hard all her life to support her family, an ordinary woman living an ordinary life. And yet, there was something rather extraordinary about her. She carried herself like a lady, despite wearing shabby, second-hand clothes and having barely a penny to spare every week after feeding her family of five hungry boys. Her husband was a proud man too, a gentle giant who looked older than his fifty-five years due to his hard life working on the docks. He was still very handsome though, a man who could still make her heart flutter, a man she would love to her dying day.

"I suppose since I was about ten or eleven. When I first heard you all talking about me being different, being short."

Her heart broke for her boy as she replied.

"Oh love, we were just joking. Of course you're one of us. You've only got to look in the mirror to see that. You're the spitting image of your dad and your brothers, just not quite as tall. But I've always said that what you lack in height, you more than make up for in good manners and charm. It will be a lucky girl who gets you as a husband one day."

"But why did you always say I was born on the wrong side of the blanket? Doesn't that make you sound like you're a bit of a scarlet woman?"

Her laugh filled the small kitchen.

"Oh Eustace, I can't believe you have been worrying about this for all these years. It was just a joke. Your dad knows that I've never had eyes for anyone but him. I fell for him when I was just a girl of sixteen and have never wanted anyone else. Your dad is a king in my eyes.

Actually, I remember now - that's when we started talking like that, joking about people being born on the wrong side of the blanket.

Old King Edward VII, God rest his soul, was such an old devil, always having one mistress or another: Sarah Bernhardt, Lillie Langtry, or that Alice Keppel. The poor old queen; I don't know how she managed to keep her head up all those years. He cheated on her so many times, and so publicly, too. His old mum, Queen Victoria, would have turned in her grave to see how badly he treated his wife. So I guess we ordinary folk started joking about it, 'cos it was too embarrassing to think about the king - our king - behaving in such a way.

It was just a joke lad, and I'm so very sorry it has worried you so much all these years. Course you're one of us. Just wait till I tell your dad, he'll be mortified."

Following this conversation, Eustace made up his mind. Now that he knew he wasn't illegitimate, that he would always have a family to come back to, it was time for him to explore the world.

"But why do you have to go? I thought we were getting on so well. I thought we had plans for the future."

Lou hadn't stopped crying since he told her about his plan to take a job on one of the big ships that came into the docks every day - the docks where he had spent the six years since he left school unloading their cargo. Six long, back-breaking years. He didn't exactly *hate* working at the docks. The camaraderie between his workmates was great, they laughed and joked all day long. But the work was hard. Being outside in all weathers, lifting heavy crates, never earning more than a few measly bob. By the time he had given his mum most of it for his board and lodging, there was hardly enough left to have a few pints on a Friday night - and certainly not enough to buy any of the smart clothes he lusted after. In his head, Eustace was something of a fashion plate, but sadly, he didn't have the income to support such dreams. He watched with envy as the rich blokes came to the docks to check on their shipments and supervise their transport to the huge warehouses that lined the river. They all wore such fancy clothes, rich man's clothes. Eustace always felt that he would look just as good, if not better than some of those toffs, if only he could afford such finery.

If he stayed in Southwark, in the place he most loved in the world, he knew he would never achieve his dreams. No, the only way to make his fortune was to become a merchant seaman, to travel the world. Of course, one day he would come back and marry this girl, this pretty girl who was sobbing loudly as they sat on the park bench.

"Oh, Lou, you know I like you. In fact, I want to do more than just like you. I want to marry you one day, but I want to be able to offer you more than just all this."

He waved his arms around, pointing at the scenery. The old brick buildings, the rather grimy cobbled streets, the stench from the river and the fish market.

People walking past stopped to stare, wondering what on earth the handsome young man was saying to upset that pretty girl so much.

"But you know I love it here. I don't ever want to leave Southwark. I'm happy here, it's enough for me."

"But Lou, you only think it's enough because you've never been anywhere else. I bet you've hardly even crossed the river, have you?" Have you ever imagined yourself somewhere hot and sunny, somewhere where people don't have to wear so many clothes just to keep warm? Where you can see nothing but countryside for miles and miles, where there aren't beggars or little orphans on every street corner, where you don't see toffs coming down to the docks to have their fun with young girls who have to sell their bodies just to put food on the table? There's a great big world out there Lou, and I want to see it. Of course I'll come back one day and settle down. Southwark will always be my home. I'm just not ready to settle yet."

She wiped her tears then stood up, with her shoulders back and her head held high.

"Okay, Eustace. If that's what you want, I hope you have a lovely time. But don't expect me to be hanging around, waiting for you to come back."

She stomped off and he stood there for ages, gazing sadly after her as she disappeared into the distance, possibly gone from him forever.

But forever is a long time, and Lou never forgot her handsome young man.

THE SAILOR RETURNS

I t was seven long years before Eustace came home from sea. At the beginning of 1913, he returned tanned, worldly wise, and more handsome than ever.

His parents were so thrilled to have him back that they organised a big party in the Bulls Head pub. They took over the upstairs room and the landlord's wife ensured there was a sufficient supply of cockles, jellied eels, whelks, and fresh bread, not to mention plenty of ale. It seemed as though the entire population of Southwark was there to welcome their boy home.

"Blimey, Lou. Isn't he handsome?"

Lou looked across the room. She could barely believe her eyes. The striking young docker she had loved when she was 16 was now an incredibly attractive man, easily as handsome as all those rich young blokes she saw hanging around the music halls.

He was surrounded by a dozen pretty young women, all leaning in as close as decency allowed to listen to his stories.

"Of course, when I was in the West Indies, it was easy to get attention. All the local ladies thought I was cute and they liked my Cockney accent."

"America is a marvellous place - lots of big buildings, taller than St. Paul's, even."

"Sometimes at sea, we'd catch a glimpse of a new place - a place we hadn't been to before. Bright blue skies and sandy beaches. Nothing in sight except for a few coconut trees."

"But I missed old Blighty. Missed seeing all you lot. I've done my travelling, seen the world, and now I'm home to stay."

As he said that, he looked across the room and the words became stuck in his throat.

"Who's that pretty girl over there? The one in the yellow dress."

Lou was wearing her new yellow dress. It was a bit fancy for just a party at the pub, but she had wanted to stand out. Even if he never noticed her, she wanted to make sure she looked and felt her best.

Her heart had started fluttering the minute she saw Eustace, even though seven long years had passed and she thought she had forgotten about him.

She had had a few boyfriends during the time he had been away, had even been quite serious about one of them and thought they might end up getting married. But the minute she spotted Eustace again, she knew she could marry no one but him. Even if he had changed and didn't like her anymore, she knew now that no one would ever take his place in her heart. If she couldn't have him, she would surely end up as a lonely old maid.

"Stand up straight, Lou, he's coming over."

For years afterwards, the couple laughed every time they thought about the next half an hour. It was as though they had suddenly been lost in their own little world.

"Hello, Lou."

"Hello, Eustace."

"How are you? I've missed you."

"I've missed you, too."

He looked down at her hands, just to be sure there was no wedding ring.

"It's been a long time."

"Yes, it has. Did you have fun?"

For a moment he was silent, his face registering a muddle of thoughts.

"Um, yes I did. But I'm glad to be home again now, and so happy to see you again, Lou."

He could never tell her about *all* his adventures. Some of them just weren't fit for the ears of nice young ladies like her. Not to mention, he certainly wouldn't be speaking of all the women he had met along the way. He had gone to sea as a boy with little to no romantic or sexual experience; he had come back a man. A man who had seen more than just a few tourist sights.

Now, standing in front of this beautiful young woman, Eustace felt like a shy young boy again. Whatever would she think of him if she knew everything he'd been up to?

"I must say, you are even more beautiful than I remembered. Could I call 'round to your place and see you next week? I've got my old job back at the docks, but I'm free every evening."

The man was as good as his word, turning up on Lou's doorstep a couple of days later clutching two big bunches of daffodils, one for her and one for her mum, Jane.

"He'll go far, that lad. Mark my words. Thinking of bringing flowers to an old lady like me, not just to his sweetheart."

In no time at all, the Plants felt like Eustace was part of the family. He spent hours chatting to Lou's dad, waiting for her to get home from work. Sometimes she had to do extra shifts at the factory, covering for some poor lass who had suddenly gone down with a dreadful disease, a broken heart, or who had gone into labour. All the girls rallied around when one had a misfortune. They had grown up together, they all knew how hard it was to survive in the slums. It was just what they did, the community was their home. It was somewhere that honestly, most of them would never leave, even if they were given the chance.

The leather factory where Lou worked was in Bermondsey.

It had been there for more than a hundred years, since the time when the area was a hub of the leather trade. There were still a few tanneries operating, although nowhere near as many as there had been in 1833 when the Leather and Skin Market had opened on Weston Street. They had since been forced to move south of the river after complaints about the noxious smells and fumes.

By the time Lou started working in the factory, the industry was in something of a decline. Many producers had moved up to the North of England, where rents and labour costs were cheaper. However, the factory she worked in survived because the owners were modern thinkers - always on the look-out for the next good thing. They had quickly realised that, although the demand for horses and saddlery was declining, the market for ladies clothing would never dry up.

So, they diversified, and alongside the bigger, more profitable items like saddles, they started a range of ladieswear: soft leather gloves, valises, even handmade shoes. Word soon got out that their leatherwork was superior, far better than some of that cheaper stuff from Leeds or Liverpool, and the company thrived. The new large department stores in the West End all clamoured to stock their goods.

"One day Lou, once we're married and settled, I want you to give up that job and just sit at home like a lady."

Lou snorted and slapped Eustace playfully on the arm.

"Not on your Nelly, Eustace. There's no way I'm going to give up my job and become a kept woman. *I'm* going to be just like all those brave suffragettes, independent and fighting for women's rights. Don't ever think you'll be able to put me in a gilded cage; I would just run away."

He smiled, ruefully. In just a couple of weeks he was going to marry this little spitfire, and he now realised that there was absolutely no way he was going to be able to restrain her, even if he wanted to. She certainly wasn't like some of the other women he had met on his travels - most of them had been so compliant, just happy to cater to his every whim as long as he looked after them financially.

What a different kind of woman altogether his Lou was.

"Oh Lou, if I'd wanted a simple, easy-going kind of wife, I certainly wouldn't be wasting my time with you! But I do have something serious I need to tell you about."

They had become engaged after just one month of getting to know each other again. Although they were both older, and in his case, much more experienced, their feelings for each other had not changed. The first walk they took together through the park had confirmed that. In no time at all, they were back to their old comfortable relationship, both relaxed and happy, thrilled to find that the old spark hadn't died. In fact, it was now a burning flame, one that neither of them could wait to enjoy on their wedding night.

"Lou, you know I can't wait to marry you, and I really do respect your feelings about waiting 'til our wedding night. But there's something serious I need to tell you. I just hope it won't make a difference as to how you feel."

He sounded so worried that she leant across the park bench on which they had been sitting (They had been sitting at a respectable distance from one another of course, in case of prying eyes - neighbours who would tell her mum and dad that she had not been behaving properly like a young, unmarried girl should! She wanted to get married without any sort of blemish on her character.).

She gave his hand a gentle squeeze, and the feeling of her small, soft hand in his big, calloused one made him falter for a moment.

"Lou, you know how much I love you, don't you?"

"Yes of course, you daft old thing! And you know I love you too, right? What's wrong?"

"Well, you know when I was away?"

"Oh, you mean when you ran away to sea and left me all alone for seven long years?"

He smiled, despite feeling anxious.

"Yep, that's what I mean."

"Eustace, you don't have to tell me everything. I'm not daft; I know that a handsome man like you didn't go seven years without *some* female company. I just don't think I want to know all the details. It's probably best if I remain in blissful ignorance."

Part of her wanted to know every little detail, everything about the different women he had known. Some of them were probably much more experienced and exotic than her. She just hoped that on their wedding night she would be able to live up to all they might have done, to provide her new husband with enough passion to keep him interested for the next fifty years.

"Oh Lou, I wish it was that simple. Trust me, none of those women could hold a candle to you. I've loved you since the first time I met you, and that won't ever change. But there is something."

She sat there with a heavy heart. Whatever was he going to tell her? Maybe he already had a wife and some children in a far-off land. But surely not? He was an honourable man, she knew he was; he would never have shirked his responsibilities like that.

"Come on, spit it out. It can't be that bad, surely?"

The park was empty. It was an early evening in December and getting chilly. Everyone was hurrying home to sit in front of their fires and shut out the winter cold.

Eustace blushed as he took off his overcoat and rolled up his shirtsleeve. Lou gasped.

"I will understand if you don't want to marry me after all. I know you won't want to look at this every day for the rest of our lives. I'm really sorry, Lou."

She laughed out loud as she looked at the top of his muscular left arm, a strong arm with glorious muscles honed from all the years working on the docks.

"Oh, Eustace. I thought it was going to be something really dreadful; I thought you were about to tell me you had some awful disease like leprosy or something."

"Aren't you a bit shocked, Lou? You seem to be taking it very well. My brothers said you'd probably have a fit and chuck the ring back at me."

She was quiet for a moment, gently stroking the little diamond engagement ring on the third finger of her left hand. In truth, she was shocked and not too happy at what she saw, but it could have been worse. He could be telling her that he already had a wife and was planning to commit bigamy when he married her on Christmas Eve.

"It happened in the West Indies. We'd all had a skinful and some of the lads wanted to go to the local brothel. I didn't want to do that, so I just sat in a bar until they'd finished, drinking far too much rum. There were a few women there, and I got chatting to a couple of them who said their uncle ran the local tattoo place. They said my mates and I should go. When the others came back they kept teasing me, saying there was something wrong with me and that I was a sissy 'cos I wouldn't go with them to the brothel. I got a bit sick of all their ribbing, so I said if they were real men they'd come to the tattoo place with me.

Well, the outshot of it was that we were all drunk - far too drunk to think properly - and so the next morning we woke up on the ship with huge hangovers and these." He pointed to his exposed arm.

Decorating his muscular bicep was a huge, gaudy tattoo, featuring a big red heart, an arrow, an anchor, and the name "ROSE."

She found herself laughing. If this was all he had to confess to, it wasn't that bad.

"Well, it wouldn't be my first choice - marrying a man with a tattoo bearing another woman's name. But I guess it'll give me something to nag you about for the rest of our days." She smiled. "Something to make our children and grandchildren realise that we weren't always boring old folk."

So, despite the odds, the couple got married on Christmas Eve as planned. Lou never told her family about the tattoo. She didn't want them judging him, best to leave it for a while! They would find out soon enough, once the weather got warmer and he took his shirt off to lie in the sunshine. That was something else they had in common; they both loved a bit of sunshine!

THE WAR

Just seven months after their wedding, in July 1914, the First World War broke out. Britain found herself at war with Germany in what was to become "the war to end all wars." It was a bloody conflict full of propaganda and wasted lives. The human suffering was great.

Women wept as their sons, eager for adventure, signed up in droves, volunteering to join the bloodbath of battle.

Jane Plant had never been more thankful she only had daughters. It was truly heartbreaking to go down to Borough Market and watch the women weeping as they told how their boys had gone to the recruiting offices and signed their lives away for King and Country.

As of March 1916, all single men between the ages of 18 and 41 were obliged to enlist. Those early volunteers were no longer enough; too many of them had been killed and the war was raging on for far longer than anyone had expected.

There were a few conscientious objectors - men who refused to fight because of personal or religious beliefs - and Jane had seen a few such men pilloried, given white feathers, or shunned for thinking war was wrong.

Many of the men the Plants knew were exempt of course, because of their work at the docks and on the river. They were considered *essential workers*, part of the war effort. Jane and others like her were so grateful their men weren't being sent overseas to become cannon fodder. Instead, they were issued with papers and badges to show they were exempt - to prove they were undertaking valuable war work. They were able to show they were working in the national interest, not just shirkers trying to protect their own skins.

Luckily for Jane, the most important man in her life, her lovely Arthur, was too old now to be sent to war.

Lots of young lads from Peabody Buildings had signed up to fight, of course. It seemed like such a big adventure, a chance to see the world. They would have the opportunity to fight for King and Country and wear a smart uniform while doing it! Everyone knew that the girls liked a man in uniform.

Eustace was not allowed to join the army.

Lou was relieved. She had already lost him for seven long years and had no intention of letting him out of her sight again.

Of course, being a young patriotic man swept up in the excitement of the whole thing, Eustace had gone along with his mates to the recruiting office in Trafalgar Square.

There they had queued for hours, hundreds of fit, young men all wanting to do their bit.

However, Eustace was never allowed to swear the oath of allegiance to the King upon the Bible. He was turned away, told he was too short. The minimum height required for a soldier was 5'3", although that was raised to 5'6" later to eliminate more people and prevent an unmanageable flood of volunteers. In later years, this height restriction was lowered once again; too many men had been lost, so even short ones were then considered by the powers that be to be suitable to sacrifice their lives.

After being rejected, Eustace continued with his daily work at the docks. All the while though, he was secretly envious as he watched many of his mates set off for war. A few times, he went to London Bridge Station to wave them off. They were all bright-eyed young men off on an adventure. Leaving their homes for the first time, wearing a brand new uniform, waving at their mothers, sisters, and sweethearts as the train pulled away.

Eustace saw women weeping, children crying, and wondered if the same was happening all over Germany. They said this was going to be the war to end wars, but could that possibly be true?

Anyway, if he was being truly honest, when it came down to it, he was glad they had stopped him from signing up. He actually had no great desire to go off fighting in some foreign land. He sometimes felt as though those seven years at sea had aged him. He had seen so much; he had no desire to go off gallivanting around the world to prove he was a hero.

Besides, his Lou needed him now more than ever. He knew she was an independent little thing, feisty and fearless, but now she was expecting their baby. It was time for her to relax a bit, he thought maybe she would slip into a more maternal role, rather than thinking she always had to stand up for women's rights.

A big smile stretched across his handsome face as he thought about his beloved wife. She was definitely the best thing that had ever happened to him.

As he hurried across the square that evening, desperate to get home to tell his wife he had been turned away and give her a hug, his mum stepped out of the shadows. He could tell she had been crying.

"Oh, Eustace. Your brothers have all gone and signed up. I suppose you knew that already. They said you'd gone with them, but your lack of height saved you. Son, suppose they all get killed. Whatever will I do?"

There was nothing he could say to make his mum feel better. It was the first time in his life he was grateful for being born a "shorty"; at least he now had a chance of surviving this bloody war, even if his brothers didn't.

The war proved to be as bloody and lengthy as they all feared. The boys who had been promised it would "all be over by Christmas" found themselves - if they were lucky enough to have made it - still fighting four years later, in foreign lands and muddy trenches, their minds and bodies forever scarred.

For the women left behind in London, life changed too.

Astrid, the second eldest Plant girl, did indeed leave home. She moved north of the river as planned, and got herself a job in a bookshop while renting a tiny garret in a rather decrepit house in Chelsea.

Despite her living situation, she was happy. Life was turning out exactly as she had imagined: no husband, no babies, a totally independent life.

Of course, she was a bit lonely at times. The house she lived in was owned by a very eccentric old lady who insisted on knocking on her door every morning at 6:30am and demanding she come down to the dusty old kitchen for a cup of tea. Although she was such a funny old girl, Astrid became rather fond of her. She regaled her family with entertaining stories of her new life every Sunday when she went back to Peabody Buildings to visit. Although she had chosen to leave, her heart and all the people she loved were still in Southwark.

For Astrid's 30th birthday in 1914, the whole family clubbed together to buy a special present for her. The world was in disarray. No one could quite believe that England was at war against Germany. It was a dreadful, dismal time - all those fine young men sent overseas and their wives and children left at home in London to fend for themselves.

Astrid had become quite vocal about women's equality, so it seemed like the perfect gift to give her... Princess Mary's Gift Book. It was a delightful anthology of short stories and poems, all beautifully illustrated by some of the most illustrious artists of the time. Authors including J.M. Barrie, Arthur Conan Doyle, and Rudyard Kipling had been among some of those happy to donate their work to such a great cause.

"All profits from sale are given to THE QUEEN'S WORK FOR WOMEN FUND, which is acting in conjunction with THE NATIONAL RELIEF FUND."

They had all been so excited to give Astrid the book and were massively rewarded when she burst into tears upon receiving it.

"Oh, thank you, thank you all so much! I just love it. I really wanted one when the first copies arrived in my bookshop, but I knew I'd never be able to afford a copy of my own. I just can't believe you got this for me. I will treasure it forever."

The whole afternoon was spent with them all poring over the book. It certainly was a very fine thing, well worth all the money they'd had to find between them to buy it.

Of course, they hadn't bought it from the bookshop where Astrid worked; that would have spoilt the surprise! Instead, Ann, the eldest Plant sister, and her husband John had taken a little trip up West. They'd had a lovely time, leaving their little son with Jane and Arthur for the day. It was a treat for them all. Little Arthur had a wonderful time being spoilt by his grandparents. He loved Grandad Arthur more than he loved anyone else in the world. The fact that they shared the same name made the old man even more special in the little boy's eyes.

Though the trip was lovely for Ann and John, there was a sadness in it, too. John had volunteered for the army and was due to join his regiment and begin training in just a few days. Now that it was really happening, now that he was going to have to leave his wife and son behind, he was beginning to doubt his decision. Perhaps he should have waited? If this war was going to be over as quickly as everyone thought, he could probably have avoided military service altogether.

He knew that Ann was cross with him for signing up, especially because he had done it without telling her beforehand. But truthfully, he had done it on a bit of a whim. All his mates at work said they were going to the recruiting office, so he just kind of tagged along. Being a tall, muscular sort of chap, he was exactly what the army was looking for. He was nothing like Lou's husband, Eustace, who failed to get in due to his height.

So overall, the day trip to get Astrid's birthday present was a kind of farewell, as well as a nice day out. They managed to find the book in a big posh bookshop on Regent Street. There were queues of people trying to buy it, and on enquiring why everyone was there at that particular time, one of the salesmen explained that it was because there had been a rumour flying around that Princess Mary herself, accompanied by her mother, the Queen, was going to be dropping in to sign a few copies.

Of course, that later proved to be untrue, just some silly nonsense put out by the publishers, Hodder and Stoughton, in an attempt to sell more books.

After buying the book, Ann and John wandered up and down Oxford and Regent Street, window shopping. They stood in front of the wonderful displays in the big windows at Selfridges for ages... If only they could afford to shop there.

They also popped into Lyons Corner House and treated themselves to a nice lunch.

On the bus home, Ann started to cry. She never cried in public, in fact, she barely ever cried at all. But now, thinking of her husband leaving so soon, she was bereft.

"Oh, John, love, whatever are me and little Arthur going to do without you? I can't bear to think of you going off to fight in some foreign land. Suppose you don't come back?"

Everyone on the bus was sympathetic to the couple's sorrow. Everyone had someone they loved who was going off to war. Everyone loved someone who might never come home.

LONDON 1918

John never did come home. He was killed in the first few months of the war - a war he had never really wanted to fight at all. Ann was widowed at the age of 35.

Fortunately, Lou and Eustace had been living in the flat with them since their wedding, so they were there to console her. They hugged Ann as she wept and took care of little Arthur when she was too distraught to care for him herself.

The whole family rallied 'round to help her during her most awful time, and the two Grannies - Mabel and Ann - took it in turns to sit with her, making sure she had plenty of cups of tea and nutritious meals to stop her from wasting away. But of course, no one could take away her heartache.

The tragedy took a toll on everyone in the family. No one knew quite what to say to help Ann through her grief. Everywhere they looked there were families like them, families grieving for young men lost to a senseless war.

As each dreadful winter passed and those soldiers spent another Christmas apart from their loved ones, the mood in the country changed. Young men were no longer clamouring to volunteer for duty; those remaining were in no hurry to join their fallen comrades and lose their life for King and Country.

By 1916, men were still being enlisted but now often against their will. Both Alice and Amy had to wave goodbye to their sweethearts, too.

Luckily, both those men came back after the war finally ended in 1918, but they came back broken, with limbs missing and minds badly affected by all they had seen on the battlefields. They married Alice and Amy on their return, but after a few years it was obvious the marriages were a mistake. The girls had not ended up with the carefree young men they had fallen in love with; instead, they found themselves living with husbands who, on the surface looked pretty much the same, but who were so much different on the inside. They had married men who were scarred forever by all they had seen. Of course, divorce was not an option - no one divorced in those days unless someone was really rich or really bad - so Alice and Amy stayed married for the next fifty years to the shells of the men they loved.

Every time Lou visited them, she felt sad for her sisters and the rather dismal lives they had. Both girls had been pretty and bright young things before the war, always happy, always enjoying their lives. Now, they were mere shadows of their previous selves. Now, it was almost as if they were actors, living in the same bodies they had always inhabited, but somehow *lesser*, trying desperately to keep up appearances of happy marriages when everyone knew they were falling apart.

As sisters, Alice and Amy were very close in adulthood - as close as they had always been growing up - and they both gave birth to three children in the next five years. The babies were beautiful and so loved. Sometimes, Lou thought that was probably the only thing that kept them both going: the love they both had for their children.

Of all the Plant sisters, Lou, Amber, and Astrid were the only ones lucky enough to have husbands who didn't go away to fight. Astrid did not have a husband at all and Lou's husband was considered too short to make a decent soldier, Amber's husband, Fred, managed to get an exemption.

No one quite knew how he had managed it, as he was a tall, fit young man in his prime, certainly strong and healthy enough to make a good fighter.

"If you ask me, that Fred's just a wide boy. I've always known he was a wrong 'un, not quite honest, if you know what I mean. I don't know how he can hold his head up 'round here, seeing all the grieving families and people who've lost husbands and sons while all the time he's swanning around town, making deals. Our Amber should be ashamed of herself, married to a dodgy bloke like that!"

But of course, Amber was not ashamed in the least. She loved the life that Fred's business ventures afforded her; it meant that she and her daughters could live a nice life in Eastbourne - in their little semi-detached villa on the seafront.

Every morning, without fail, she and her daughters took a brisk walk along the promenade and she told them daily how lucky they were to be growing up out of London, away from all the dirt, grime, and overcrowding of the slums.

However, even they weren't totally unaffected by the war.

In 1915, a camp had opened in Eastbourne to treat soldiers who had been damaged by trench warfare. It was the largest camp of its kind and was considered a great success. Of the 150,000 soldiers suffering from shell shock and the effects of gas attacks, eighty percent were treated, considered *cured*, and sent back to fight in battle. They were given blue uniforms to wear - a change from the lice-infested, blood-encrusted khaki ones they had previously worn. These "blue boys" were welcomed and treated well by the inhabitants of the little town. Because of the blue uniforms, everyone knew they were heroes, not conscientious objectors who deserved a white feather.

Amber was quite satisfied that she and Fred did their bit for the war effort by donating a bit of cash and Fred's old clothes to these men. It never occurred to either of them that the fortunes they were able to share had been made from other people's misery.

You see, without the war, Fred would never have flourished in the way he had with it. He had taken over the ownership of several small shops, which were failing due to their male owners being away, fighting. The men's wives, after struggling for a couple of years to make ends meet, were glad to hand over the responsibility to a new owner: someone who seemed to have lots of wealthy contacts and who could pay the exorbitant shop rents charged by greedy landlords. By the end of the war, Fred owned seven such shops: a couple of butchers, a bakery, two hardware stores, a tobacconist shop, and a newsagent's shop. They all turned a tidy profit, and sometimes, he even employed the previous owners to run the places for him when they returned from the war.

Amber, Fred, and the girls rarely went up to visit their family in Southwark. They felt themselves to be a little above the tenants of Peabody Buildings now; they had gone up in the world and had no intention of allowing their less well-off relatives drag them down.

THE EARLY MARRIED YEARS

L ou and Eustace settled into married life very well. They were so happy to be together, to be husband and wife at last. Of course, it wasn't exactly ideal living with Lou's sister Ann and the two grannies. It was not what they would have chosen if they had more money, but they all muddled along quite nicely.

After Ann's husband was killed, Lou was glad they were all together. It was heartbreaking to watch her sister mourn the man she had loved so dearly, and to see her little nephew cry himself to sleep at night because he missed his dad. However, she loved that she could be there for the little family in their greatest time of sorrow.

Lou lost the baby she had been expecting at the beginning of the war - the baby that she and Eustace had been so excited about.

She had been working at the glove factory when one day, one of the heavy machines toppled over, knocking her sideways. The little baby inside her did not survive the impact, and for months afterwards, even though her body healed, her mind struggled to recover.

"No Eustace, I mean it. I don't want no more babies. I can't go through this again, I just can't. Anyway, Ann and little Arthur need me now. I've got to be a mother to the little lad until Ann's well enough to do it again. Maybe I'll feel differently in a few years... then perhaps we could try again?"

After the war ended and Ann was more or less back to her old self, Lou did get pregnant again. Sadly, she lost three more babies, probably due to stress and lack of proper nourishment. She was often sickly, with a pale complexion and a dry, rasping cough.

"I'm worried about that girl, Mabel. If she loses any more babies I think she might lose her mind. It's so hard for her, seeing all the other young mothers in the square, pushing their babies 'round so proudly. And of course, her sisters manage to pop out babies as easily as shelling peas. She doesn't say much, but I can see how much it hurts her."

The two grannies, Ann and Mabel, were sitting in their usual places in front of the roaring coal fire.

"I know, Ann. It breaks my heart too, but what can we do to help her?"

"Well, I think we should suggest that she give up her job at the leather factory. Being in that place with all those fumes and dust flying around can't be good for her."

Ann spoke quietly, but with a steeliness in her voice. She could remember so clearly back to when she was a young girl and had been forced to take a job at the glove factory, to earn enough money to support herself after her father had died and her mother had been committed to the lunatic asylum.

"Those places just aren't very healthy, Mabel. I remember when I sometimes had to visit the tanneries in Bermondsey to pick up some new bits of leather. They always seemed like hell holes to me - horrible, smelly places. I know they've probably improved a bit over the years, but I still don't think they're a good place for our Lou to work."

Lou, being the strong, feisty girl she was, just brushed off their worries.

"Don't worry, you two. I'm fine. I like working there! I earn pretty good money and it gives me something to think about, sewing fancy goods all day. I think I'd go mad if I had to stay at home all day with you lot!"

She was putting on a brave face. In reality, the leather factory work was hard. She often had to cart big piles of hides from one side of the huge room to the other, and sometimes the smell was pretty awful from the tannery. But she did like the work; it was good to create something beautiful from a flat piece of leather and she loved the camaraderie of the place, working with young men and women she had known all her life. Of course, during the war years, there hadn't been many young men on the factory floor. The place was made up of old men, girls like her, and the odd, misfit men who weren't considered *good enough* to be cannon fodder.

Lou winced when people talked about "cowards and conscientious objectors." She had seen enough white feathers being given out. Someone had even tried to give one to her Eustace once when he turned up for work on the docks.

The war years had been hard on them all, but at least most of the family had come through relatively unscathed.

In December 1922, three years after the end of the war, Lou was pregnant again. This time, everything went well. Much to the delight of the whole family, baby Benjamin was born, safe and sound.

Benjamin was a beautiful baby, the spitting image of his mother, and Eustace was the proudest father that Peabody Buildings had ever seen. He strutted around the place like a peacock, telling everyone who was willing to listen about his *"wonderful wife, the best and bravest ever."* He could be heard exclaiming, *"my boy, you wouldn't believe how bright and handsome he is, definitely the best baby that's ever been born on this earth!"*

People smiled when he bragged about his little family. After all this young couple had been through, losing so many babies, it was time they had some joy in their lives.

Baby Benjamin, who quickly became known as just Ben, brought the whole family nothing but joy. By the time he was a year old he was walking and talking - baby talk of course, nothing that most people would consider "conversation," but to his besotted parents he was a genius, a wonder boy who would go on to achieve great things.

He was joined four years later by a little brother. Whereas young Ben had a thick head of straight, dark hair, his new sibling was born with a shock of blonde, almost white curls.

He was named Dennis - an unusual choice and a name not often heard in Southwark. Eustace had met an old sailor in the pub one Friday night and had rather liked his name.

Lou, always one to enjoy shocking people, had thought it was perfect, a good foil to the rather sensible name they had given their firstborn son.

The two young boys thrived. They were loved by so many people, their immediate family of course, and most of the inhabitants of Peabody Buildings. There were a *few* grumpy old ones, people who didn't like children at all and who complained constantly about the mess and noise they caused, but they were in the minority. Almost everyone in Southwark loved Ben and Dennis.

Lou and Eustace were never short of willing babysitters. Grannies, great-grannies, aunties, and cousins. Everyone wanted to look after the two delightful little boys.

All was well until two days after little Dennis's second birthday.

Lou and Eustace would never forget that dreadful, dark day, the day their lives changed forever.

THE NEXT FEW YEARS

I t took three long years before they could talk about him without crying.

Their little blonde boy, the baby of the family.

He had so enjoyed his birthday celebrations. They had made a fuss of him, wrapped up a few small presents, and Lou had even gone to the trouble of making a cake.

"Blimey, Lou, that's the first time I've ever seen you make a cake."

"And it even tastes alright!"

"Dennis, what have you done to turn your mum all domesticated? You must be a special boy!"

"It's not fair, Mum, you didn't make <u>me</u> a cake on <u>my</u> birthday."

Ben was right. She hadn't made him a cake, but somehow she had just felt the urge to do one for little Dennis, to make his birthday really special.

Afterward, she was so glad she had done that.

Two days after Dennis's second birthday - two days after the nice little celebration they'd held for him, he was dead.

Killed by the dreaded diphtheria. Gone in a flash, almost before his loving family's very eyes.

If only they had been rich people, then they could have afforded a doctor. Instead, they had dilly-dallied, worried about spending their last sixpence on calling out the doctor and instead just praying the little boy was going to get better. Deep down, they knew from bitter experience that too many infants died in the slums from a lack of money, but they had never in a million years thought it would happen to one of their own. Their little Dennis.

A GRAND DAY OUT

I n the photo, Arthur senior, Eustace, and little Ben were
all staring at the camera. Ben, aged six, was sitting in between his father and grandfather, wearing a long-sleeved
white shirt with elastic braces holding up his knee-length
dark shorts, shorts that showed off his spindly little legs and
knobby knees.

Both the men were wearing their best Sunday suits.

Arthur, who was still handsome and rather distinguished
despite his advancing years and bald pate, stared directly at
the camera, his big, capable hands resting on his lap. He was
a tall, good-looking man, with kind eyes.

On the other side of little Ben was his father. Eustace was
another good-looking man, although somewhat shorter than
his father-in-law. In the photo, he was wearing a dark suit with
a black armband sewn onto it. Still in mourning, not just for
little Dennis, but also for his old dad who had recently died.

They were sitting on the sea wall, the rather choppy looking ocean and majestic white cliffs in the background. All
three of them were squinting a little in the bright sunshine,
trying to smile for the camera. The picture was taken by one of

those professional street photographers, persuasive men who seemed to lurk on every street corner and every seaside promenade, trying to convince people to have their likenesses made.

"You won't regret it, guv. Something to look back on for years to come. Something to remind you of that happy day."

Over the years, Eustace reckoned he must have spent a small fortune on these kinds of photos. His Lou loved having her picture taken; she used to wait anxiously for them to arrive in the post or to get a message that they had been processed and were ready to be collected from the photographer's studio. She would hurry along there, excited to see the end result.

She was never disappointed. Lou was very photogenic, as were most of her good-looking family members. Consequently, the mantelpiece in their little flat was covered in black and white and sepia photos, all in little wooden frames.

This time though, Lou had refused to pose for the picture. She was still grieving and knew she didn't look her best, even though she realised the value of the photos. Since their little Dennis had passed away, she knew all she had left of him were a half a dozen photos, pictures of her little angel with his mass of curly hair.

He looked so alive, so cheeky in each shot. It broke her heart to look at them and realise what she'd lost.

Truthfully, she had never realised that losing a child would hurt so much. Of course she had lost babies before, but they had been through miscarriages. They were babies who died before they had a chance to draw their first breath. While she had still been heartbroken in those times, while she cried for months over each of her lost babies, this was worse. To have given birth to a child, to have nurtured and loved him for two years just to have him snatched away with almost no warning was more than she could bear. She went into a deep decline, a decline approaching madness - something she seemed to have no control over.

Everyone tried to help her, of course. They all crowded into the little flat on a daily basis, desperate to ensure Lou was never alone to do something silly.

They all knew that losing a child sometimes made women lose their minds completely. There had been several cases where women from Peabody Buildings, finding their grief too much too bear, had thrown themselves from the roof onto the hard concrete square below. Others had thrown themselves into the River Thames late at night, when there were few people around and the chances of being fished out of the cold water and rescued were slim. A couple of others had been declared insane and sent to the local asylum.

Lou was luckier than them. She had a big loving family who ensured that no such harm came to her. They watched over her day and night. Slowly, after several months of constant weeping, she began to come back to life a little.

"Dad, why does Mum cry all the time?"

Eustace put his arm 'round the little boy. He was too choked up to speak for a moment or two.

"Oh, Ben, she's just sad about losing our Dennis. She loved your little brother so much. We all did."

"I loved him too, Dad. I was going to start teaching him things like how to count to twenty, roll marbles, and play hopscotch. Now he's gone. Will you get me another little brother?"

Eustace looked down at his eldest son. Now, his only son. He patted the little boy's head gently.

"I don't know, son. You can't just replace people, especially lovely ones like our Dennis."

Eustace's heart was breaking too. He had loved both his boys equally, but he knew that Lou had had a soft spot for their youngest one. Now he was in heaven and Lou was in utter despair.

"Did Mum like our Dennis better than me?" The little boy's voice was rather forlorn.

"Course not, lad. You're both our special precious boys and of course, we love you the same."

Eustace was aware that he was using the present tense by saying "love," rather than *loved*.

"But I heard Mum telling Granny Jane that he was her golden boy, the best of us. And that no one would ever take his place in her heart."

"Oh, Ben. She didn't mean that she loved him more than you. It's just that sometimes, when you lose people you love, you want to remember them always, remember how very special they were. That's what your mum was talking about. Just her way of remembering our little Dennis."

The little boy nodded, then ran outside to play with his mates in the square.

Eustace stood quietly for a moment, watching his son run out into the sunshine. He was such a gentle, kind lad, a rather quiet boy with deep feelings. They would have to keep a careful eye on him.

"Lou my darling, I'm a bit worried about our Ben."

Lou looked up from the book she was reading. It was one Astrid had brought her. Another novel, another love story. Something to take her mind off the awfulness around her. Something to distract her mind from the dark thoughts she had been having ever since the dreadful morning when they had lowered her angel's tiny body into the ground at Nunhead Cemetery. She still had the little black-edged burial card propped up on the mantelpiece next to her favourite photo of him. Soon, when the ground had settled enough, she and Eustace planned to get the stonemasons down the Elephant and Castle to make them a nice little angel to go on top with their boy's name engraved on the marble base.

"Is he alright? Is he hurt?"

"No love, he's not hurt. But he is hurting. It breaks my heart. He's grieving for his little brother, too, but I think somehow we've forgotten that a bit. He told me just now that he missed Dennis. He said he was about to start teaching him how to count and play marbles."

"Oh, Eustace."

She burst into tears and he crossed the room to comfort her. He couldn't remember one day in the last six months when she hadn't cried, and now, just when she seemed to be turning a corner, he had set her off again.

It had been Lou's idea to go to the seaside.

"I think our lad needs a treat, something to take his mind off everything." She didn't add that she too needed a treat, although "treat" seemed rather too flippant a word. How could she even think of enjoying herself when her little boy, her precious little Dennis, was lying in the ground?

"Why don't we go down to Dover? That would make for a nice day out. We could get the bus or the train, take a few bits to eat and a flask of tea, and Ben and Arthur could explore the castle and see all the big boats. If it's a nice day, we might even see across to France. Some of the family might fancy coming too!"

In the end there were a few of them who went on the trip. Lou, Eustace, Ben, Jane and Arthur Plant, Ann and little Arthur Jr., even Astrid decided to take a day off of work and join them.

"I've never been to Dover and I think it will do me good to get some sea air. I might even get a bit of inspiration for my next book!"

Astrid had recently decided to become an author. She was surrounded by books all day long at the bookshop and had been inspired and encouraged by the old lady she lived with - who, it turned out, had been a fairly successful writer in her youth (albeit under a male pen name). It seemed that in those long-ago days before women got the right to vote, people would often dismiss a woman's writing as frothy or inadequate, certainly not worthy of publication.

In the end, after much discussion, they decided to go to Dover by train.

"I reckon we should take the train. If we go by bus, the kids will only nag about going on the top deck, and I don't fancy going all that way with a cold wind blowing my hair about."

Ann had just gotten her hair done in the latest bob cut, a new fashion trend that had some of the old folk tearing their hair out.

Granny Mabel was absolutely distraught. "Oh my gawd. Have you seen our Ann's new haircut? I bet all the girls in the Buildings will start to copy her now. I'm not sure if I like it; it's not very ladylike. And have you noticed the way these young ones are wearing shorter skirts and no corsets? I reckon it will come to no good. Showing off too much of their legs will give blokes the wrong idea. In my day, we hardly let them get a glimpse of our ankles!"

"Oh Gran, don't be such an old fusspot. You were young once, and I bet your mum and dad didn't approve of all your goings on."

Granny Mabel and Granny Ann exchanged knowing smiles. Although their lives had started out so differently, what with Mabel being practically brought up on the fish stall at Borough Market and Ann having a more genteel existence in leafy Islington, they both knew that every generation of kids had its moments, its wild times that parents naturally disapproved of.

"Actually, my girl, I'm not an old fusspot. Just someone who's been around a bit longer than you and understands the world better."

Everyone in the crowded kitchen smiled. Once Granny Mabel got on her high horse, there was no stopping her.

"You youngsters think you know everything. You think that we old ones have never lived, never been through anything. Well, let me tell you my girl, I know more than you give me credit for. Before you was even a twinkle in your dad's eye, I had seen more of the world than you could ever imagine... even though I never left Southwark."

It was true. She had spent her whole existence in a place where life passed through. Birth, marriage, disease, death. Ships carrying men and cargo from all over the world. Foreign sailors down at the docks who had always been happy to chat with the bright-eyed little girl as she collected the day's catch from the fishing boats. Mabel had been round-eyed with wonder as the sailors told her of the exotic places and people they had met during their travels. Then they would hurry off 'round the corner to visit the little brothel run by old Ma Wiggins. Mabel had also been through the Great War, seeing all the misery and despair it caused. How dare these chits of girls presume she knew nothing?

In a way, everyone in the family was glad that she was talking to Ann like that. For too many years, they had all pussy-footed around her, desperately trying not to upset the young widow. But now, so many years after that dreadful war ended, their Ann had adjusted to her new normal. It was often as if she was her old sunny self, and little Arthur Jr. was thriving.

"Actually, you lot, I agree with our Ann. I reckon we should go on the train. That would make it a real adventure, a really grand day out."

Arthur Plant rarely made any decisions. Usually he just did what his wife and daughters told him to do. He had learnt long ago that when you live in a house full of women, it was much better to try and keep the peace rather than rock the boat!

"Oh Dad, what a great idea. I've never been on a train."

"Well, as you know, your mum and I caught the train when we went down to Eastbourne to visit our Amber last year and we thoroughly enjoyed it, didn't we Jane?"

His wife beamed at him and nodded her head.

"We certainly did, love. It was smashing. Yes, I think it's a great idea."

"I think we can get on at Blackfriars and go straight through. I'll check it out tomorrow. Mind you, it won't be cheap for us all to go, but it will be grand. Like a little holiday."

And so they did take the train. What an adventure they had.

Everyone dressed in their Sunday best - the men wearing their suits with open-neck shirts. They wore their vests underneath the shirts, and old Arthur also popped a jumper under his suit jacket, just in case it was a bit chilly at the seaside.

The ladies wore their best dresses and carried hand-knitted cardigans. The two boys, Arthur Jr. and Ben, wore long-sleeved, open-necked shirts with knee-length shorts and braces.

Spirits were high as the family left the comfort of the train. They had had the carriage almost to themselves and been able to stare out of the windows for the whole journey, marvelling at all the fields, farms, and little villages as they whizzed past.

"It's just so different from Southwark, isn't it? I bet these people wish they lived in the bright lights like us. I would hate not having many neighbours; who on earth would you chat with all day?"

"Well, I love it. I reckon I'm going to be a farmer and live in the country one day. I could keep cows, sheep, and chickens. And I would marry a pretty girl like my mum and have six children to help me on the farm."

They all smiled at little Arthur. Despite losing his dad at such a young age, he had inherited many of his fine qualities. He was gentle, quiet, and kind, a thoughtful and caring boy.

"Oh don't be daft, Arthur. When we grow up, you should stay in Southwark and we could open a bookshop together. Aunty Astrid would help us. Wouldn't you?"

Astrid looked at the two bright-eyed little boys sitting opposite her.

"Well, if you two rascals ever grow up to be sensible men, not silly little boys who fight over every board game, then I reckon I will be happy to help you. We could call it

"The Plants' Place - The best bookshop in South London!"

"Oh Aunty Astrid, that won't do." Arthur looked close to tears.

"Why not, Arthur?"

"Because I'm not a Plant. My dad's name was John West, so that means I'm a West, not a Plant."

"Oh, don't be silly. Of course you're a Plant. Just because your dad had a different name doesn't mean you're not one of us. Anyway, when you grow up, you can always change your name to Arthur Plant-West. Then people will think you're really posh!"

Dover was just as wonderful as they all hoped. They sat on the old sea wall and ate their pies, little triangles of pastry filled with carrot, onion, and suede. They had hoped to add a bit of minced meat or some fish, but the train fares had taken all their spare cash. It didn't matter though, they were content just to be on their adventure together. There was plenty of tea to drink; they had brought four big flasks and Arthur had promised that if they all behaved themselves, he would treat them to an ice cream before they caught the train back to London. One of his mates at the docks had told him about a new ice cream parlour on the seafront in Dover, a smashing place apparently, run by some Italian immigrants. *"You won't regret it, mate. Best ice cream I've ever tasted in my life. Worth every penny."*

So Arthur had saved all his spare pennies, and now they jingled comfortingly in his jacket pocket. How excited those kids were going to be to have a real Italian ice cream!

Lou felt herself relaxing as the day went on. Of course being surrounded by her loving family made it easier - easier to not feel quite so guilty about enjoying herself when her dead baby couldn't. She knew it was time to start snapping out of it, to stop indulging her grief, but somehow, she couldn't. Every time she thought about that little white coffin being lowered into the ground...

"Mum, Mum, come and look at this."

Ben was pointing out to sea, looking at all the boats bobbing around in the harbour.

"Dad says that some of those boats go all the way to France. All the time. Every day. Can you believe that, Mum? Fancy being able to cross that big wide ocean in one day and end up in a different country. I wish I could do that one day. Visit a different country."

His dad ruffled his hair.

"And I just love the way the wind messes my hair up. I love the seaside. Can Arthur and I make some sandcastles while you're all drinking your tea?"

It was a very happy day for them all. They were absolutely exhausted by the time they got back to Peabody Buildings.

FEELING BETTER

"Eustace?"

"Yes, love?"

"I was thinking about getting a job."

"Why on earth do you want a job, love? I thought you were happy here all day, keeping the place nice and chatting away with your mum and grannies and all your mates."

"Well, our Ben is at school all day. Ann isn't here either now, as she's just started at the biscuit factory. Plus, I get a bit fed up just hanging 'round the square gossiping all day. Sometimes I wish I was back at the glove factory. I really loved it there, you know that. I don't reckon it's fair that we women have to give up our jobs just 'cos we get married. Those suffragettes were fighting for us to have equal rights, to be as good as any man."

Eustace knew it must be serious if Lou was bringing up the suffragettes. She and Astrid always brought them into the conversation when they were trying to make an important point.

"Ann says they're looking for more workers at the biscuit factory. They lost so many blokes during the war that now they're taking on more women - and not just for the boring, simple jobs either. And she says they're happy to take on married women, as long as their kids are over five and at school all day. They won't consider anyone with little 'uns; they reckon they take too much time off when their babies get sick."

She paused, letting the information sink in.

"Now, I know you provide for us really well. Ben and I never want for nothing, but if I got a little job it would help a bit. Give us a few extra shillings for luxuries."

"Oh Lou, do you really think it's a good idea? Won't you be too tired to look after us properly if you go out to work?"

As soon as the words left his lips, he realised his mistake.

She stood up, put her hands on her hips and glared across at him.

"Oh, so now you're going to act like the Victorian husband, are you? Don't you realise those stuffy old values died out after the war? Women go to work everywhere now. Modern husbands don't make a fuss; they just encourage their wives."

Two weeks later, Lou set off for her first shift at the Peek, Frean, and Co., a biscuit factory in Bermondsey. She was so excited as she walked along the cobbled streets, arm in arm with her sister.

"Blimey Ann, I never thought I'd be doing this again after all these years, turning up to a factory whistle going off. I loved being at home with the boys, but they don't need me there all day anymore. This will fill that gap very nicely."

She still referred to her "boys" in conversation. Anyone who didn't know her story always assumed she was a mother to at least two sons, and she never corrected them. In her head, her Dennis still lived. She couldn't bear to think of his little body rotting away in the ground, so instead he lived within her, never growing up, always remaining her golden baby with the blonde curls.

"I loved working at the leather factory, but I think I'm going to love this place just as much... once I get used to the work and get to know a few people. Oh look, isn't that old Betty Smith over there? I didn't realise she worked here."

It took Lou no time at all to settle in. After just two weeks, it felt like she'd been there forever. Having been used to factory work, she found the job easy. It was pretty light work, much easier than carrying big piles of cow hides from one side of a factory floor to the other. She grew to love her workmates, mostly women from the same neighbourhood - from the mean streets of the slums. And of course, she loved the extra few shillings she was able to add to the family budget every week. Her Eustace had always earned a good wage; he had been promoted down at the docks, so he brought in a decent bit of money every week. His wage was enough to pay their rent and put food on the table, but now they would be able to have a few extras - maybe even an occasional ice cream like those delicious ones they'd had in Dover. A new ice cream kiosk had just opened near Borough Market, run by some Italian immigrants. They were nice people. Their kids went to the same school as Ben and Arthur, and a couple of times they had come 'round to the square to play football with the other boys.

* * *

The years ticked by, as they always do, filled with the usual amount of family dramas, despair, and death.

The Roaring Twenties were in full swing. Now, all the young women - and many of the older ones - had shortened their skirts, chopped off their long hair, and thrown away their horrible, constricting laced corsets. Marcel waves, short bobs, flapper dresses, and the Charleston quickly became the order of the day.

"C'mon, Eustace. Let's get Ann to babysit while we go to the Palais. She won't mind, she doesn't like dancing anyway. She'd much rather sit at home and read a good book."

Friday and Saturday night dances were all the rage now, and lots of dance halls had sprung up all over London, catering to the new craze.

"Old Betty at work reckons that new place is the bees knees, it's got a great dance floor and sells good beer."

She had slipped in the bit about the beer knowing that might sway him.

"Oh love, do we have to? You know I always like to take it easy at the weekend. I don't finish work 'til midday on Saturdays, then I like to come home and put my feet up, maybe read the paper."

She snorted. "Oh no. You're turning into a real old man. Even my *dad* would go dancing if mum asked him to, and he's really old."

"Oh, Lou."

"Don't you 'Oh, Lou' me! I know for a fact that if one of your mates suggested a Saturday night drink at the pub, you'd be gone like a shot. The least you can do is take me dancing, and I won't take no for an answer. All the girls from the factory are going with their blokes... I expect they could find a spare one for me if you're not willing!"

Eustace jumped out of the chair he had been lounging in and threw his arms around her.

"Blimey, if you think I'm going to let another bloke have you dancing in his arms, you're wrong, missus. You're my Lou and always will be. What time do we have to go?"

She smiled to herself as he held her tightly. He really was the loveliest man, but so easy to tease. As if she would ever go off without him! Sure, she might go to the odd dance or even to the pictures with a girlfriend, but she would always much rather go with him. He was her best friend, the father of her sons.

"Just 'cos you've got that tattoo that says 'Rose' on your arm doesn't mean you can forget you've got a wife called Lou, whom you have to keep happy."

They both laughed. His tattoo had been a constant source of teasing since she saw it for the first time. Every time he had upset her over the years, she brought it up. She had never spoken in malice, but he was always aware that she hated it. She hated being reminded that he'd had any kind of a history before he came back to her.

"Dad, why does that thing on your arm say 'Rose,' when mum's name is Louisa?"

Neither of them had been aware that Ben was standing there in the kitchen doorway. He was such a well-behaved, quiet lad that he often went unnoticed.

Eustace could feel Lou tense slightly in his arms, unaware of how he was going to respond to their son. It was the first time Ben had mentioned the tattoo, although he had obviously been aware of it for years.

"Well, lad. One day, a very, very long time ago, when I was a sailor at sea..."

Ben stood, entranced. He loved listening to all the stories his dad told.

"... after a particularly bad crossing - one where we nearly all drowned in our beds 'cos the waves were so big -"

"I thought you said you slept in hammocks, not beds?"

"Yes, of course lad, you're quite right... hammocks. Anyway, this particular day, once we landed on terra firma..."

"What's terra firma, Dad?"

"Terra firma means solid, dry land. Don't they teach you anything at that school of yours?"

Eustace was stalling for time, trying desperately to come up with a story that would placate the boy without allowing him to judge his dad too harshly.

"Anyway, we landed in this place called the West Indies."

"Is that next door to India?"

"No lad, it's in the Caribbean - where lots of the sugar and fancy fruit we unload at the docks comes from. Are you going to stop interrupting so I can get on with my story?"

Lou released herself from his arms and slumped into the old armchair. She would need a comfy seat to relax in to hear this tall story.

"Well, this particular day was hot and sunny. The sun was high in the sky and everywhere we looked there were beautifully-coloured flowers. Not flowers like they have down the market, but big, exotic ones in shades of red, orange, and yellow. I could hardly take my eyes off them. They were so lovely, just like your mum."

He looked down at Lou as he said this and wished he hadn't. The look on her face was priceless. He knew she was enjoying his discomfort. Any minute now, she would burst out laughing.

He really didn't want to mention any of the beautiful women he had met on that island. He had only been a lad, after all, and a fairly innocent and naïve one at that. Away from home for the first time in his life, living and working with men much older and more worldly than him. He certainly wasn't going to tell his son about how he had stayed up drinking rum in the bar all afternoon while his mates trooped off to the local brothel. Let the lad keep his innocence for as long as possible.

"Come on, Eustace. Explain your tattoo to our boy."

He could hear the laughter in his wife's voice.

"Well, as I've said, it was a nice sunny day, so we set off to explore the town. It was only a small place - nowhere near as big as Southwark - but much hotter and a bit exotic."

"What does 'exotic' mean, Dad?"

Eustace sighed. This was turning into something much longer and more drawn out than he wanted. And of course *she,* his beloved wife, wasn't helping much. She was just sitting there, enjoying every second of his squirming.

"'Exotic' means different, unusual, foreign."

"Oh, okay."

"So, we was just minding our business, strolling around the town, looking in the little shops, buying a few trinkets to take home for our mums and sisters."

"Didn't you buy anything for Mum?"

Lou intervened, suddenly feeling a bit sorry for her husband now that he was being cross-examined by their son.

"Oh, Ben, Dad didn't know he was going to end up marrying me. He didn't realise he was going to be lucky enough to land the prettiest girl in Southwark when he came home from sea and stopped being a sailor."

That shut both her menfolk up for a few minutes, each reflecting on her words.

Eustace was the first one to speak again. "So, as I was saying before I got so *rudely* interrupted by you two, there we was, minding our own business, when this bloke came up and asked us if we wanted to go back to his place to sample the local specialities."

"What's 'local specialties,' Dad?"

Lou couldn't stop her laughter from escaping, but she attempted to cover it by pretending to have a coughing fit.

"Um, well it just means local stuff like fruits, flowers, veg, and all that. Oh, and we saw a few brightly-coloured parrots, too. We taught them a bit of cockney. You should have heard them repeat it in their funny little squawks: *"Oh gor blimey guv,"* and *"Is it time to go up the apples and pears?"*

"Is that when you got your tattoo? That's very brightly coloured, too."

"Yes, that's right lad."

Eustace had always been very embarrassed about his tattoo. The only people who sported such things were old sailors, and now it marked him as an old sailor, too. His mum and sisters had been horrified when he returned to London with it - a bright, gaudy thing engraved with a woman's name. A woman he couldn't even remember.

"Sometimes, lad, we do silly things. I wasn't always this boring old man who worked on the docks and read the paper every night. Once, a long time ago, I was a silly young man - only about ten years older than you are now - and I made a few mistakes. Like this tattoo."

"But why does it say 'Rose,' when mum's name is Louisa? Why didn't you marry Rose if you liked her enough to have her name drawn on your arm?"

That completely undid Lou. Leaping up from her chair, she enfolded her son in her arms, kissing the top of his head gently.

"Oh, Ben, if your dad had known he was going to be lucky enough to end up with us lot, he'd have gotten an even *bigger* tattoo to fit 'LOUISA,' 'BEN,' and 'DENNIS.' It would have taken up half his arm!"

Eustace smiled gratefully. Their boy seemed happy enough with her explanation, and he suddenly wriggled out of his mum's embrace to ask if he could go outside to play football.

Eustace relaxed.

"Oh, love. Thank you. I was struggling a bit trying to come up with an excuse."

He embraced her, knowing what it had cost her to mention little Dennis's name. He knew that she still grieved for her youngest son.

THE 1930S

Londonin the early 1930s was a good time to be alive.

The people had survived the World War and the dockers' strike of 1920, and luckily had not yet been quite as affected by the Great Depression as their fellow humans in America had been.

The docks were thriving, the Port of London being one of the largest ports in the whole world.

Down at the Surrey Commercial Docks, where Eustace worked, things were good. He had received yet another promotion and was now working as a dock checker - an inspector of sorts. He was happy in his work *and* happy in his marriage.

But of course, like all families, they too had suffered some losses.

Eustace's old mum had managed to keep going until well into her eighties, although by the end, she had been almost blind and very deaf.

Lou had lost both her precious grandmas, gone within a couple of days of each other. Both were killed by the awful influenza that was running rife through the city.

Granny Ann had gone as she had lived, quietly and with dignity. The girl from Islington, the daughter of an immigrant silk weaver,, a woman who had gone on to become a matriarch of a big London Cockney family.

Then there was Granny Mabel, who had also died as she lived. Loud and dramatic to the end.

The family grieved them both equally. Life would not be the same without the old pair sitting on their matching wooden chairs in front of the fire.

They had become such good friends in later life - closer even than sisters - that the family decided to give them a joint funeral.

"It's what they would have wanted. Just think how happy they'd be, looking down on us making all these arrangements in their honour."

In the end, it had been a grand funeral, one of the grandest that the streets of Southwark had ever seen. The family had hired a couple of glass carriages, one for each oak coffin. Each carriage was drawn by a pair of huge, black horses, sporting black feather plumes. Two undertakers wearing top hats and frock coats walked slowly in front of the carriages and the family followed at a respectful distance. People lined the cobbled streets - all wearing black armbands - and every man doffed his cap as the procession passed.

As they neared Borough Market, a small cheer went up. *"God bless two great ladies, they'll be sadly missed."* Then *the* crowd went quiet, removing their hats and bowing their heads as the carriages went by.

Lou was glad to see how much her two grannies had been loved. Of course the family had loved them, but until today, she had never realised quite how much everyone else had, too. What a wonderful thing, to have lived such a simple life and yet, to have left such a great mark.

* * *

"I just wish we didn't have to share our washing facilities with the whole building or go to the bathhouse every week. I much preferred it when us girls all used to go in the old tin bath in front of the fire every Sunday. I miss those days."

"Oh Lou, what do you expect me to do about it? You know that's how most people in London live. Unless they're rich, then they can have as many indoor lavs and bathrooms as they'd like."

"Can you imagine though, Eustace, how lovely it would be to have your own private bathroom? Somewhere you could strip off and have a good wash without half your neighbours peeping at you."

"Stop dreaming, girl. That's never gonna happen to us. Well, not unless I win a few quid on the horses... and you know I'm not really a betting man."

They had just returned from a weekend visiting Lou's sister, Amber, in Eastbourne.

"Our Amber says it's a marvellous feeling to do your washing in your own copper boiler in your own kitchen, then put it through your own wringer before pegging it on the line in your own backyard. Her Fred has even made her a wooden prop and a nice little stool to put the washing basket on so she doesn't have to bend down."

Eustace raised his eyebrows. If he heard one more thing about how marvellous his brother-in-law was, he just might erupt. He couldn't believe how Lou had been so impressed by that slimy little toad. Everyone knew he was no good, a real Jack the Lad, a wide boy. Lou typically talked about what a rotter he was, even if he did provide their Amber and her daughters with a nice little home and plenty of luxuries.

"But would you really want to be stuck down there, away from all the family? Your Amber seemed really pleased to see us. She never used to seem to care about us much, but I got the feeling this time that she really enjoyed our company. Maybe things aren't as rosy between her and Fred as she'd have us all believing."

"Well, I'm not saying I want to live by the seaside. But I would like my own bathroom. And maybe a little garden. Then you could grow some nice fresh vegetables."

Eustace was sitting at the old kitchen table, engrossed in the newspaper.

"Why have you suddenly taken to reading *The Times*, love? Isn't that a bit posh for a working man like you?"

"Oh Lou, one of the bosses gave it to me today after he'd finished reading it. He said that he knew I was quite smart and he thought I might like to try my hand at this new fangled crossword thing they've just started publishing."

It was true that Eustace was quite smart. That was why he was getting such rapid promotions at work; the men in charge could see that he had a good, quick brain. They could see he was intelligent, even though he had not had much formal education.

"Here, let me have a look."

She sat beside him at the table for fifteen minutes, screwing up her pretty face in concentration.

"Blimey, Eustace, how do you ever work out what all these squares are supposed to say? I can't even think of one answer. Ben, did you realise your dad was a genius?"

The boy looked at his dad and smiled before replying.

"Yes, Mum. I always knew Dad was clever. That's the only reason I do so well at school, 'cos he always helps me with my homework. Sometimes, when you're home late from the factory, me and dad sit at this table and he helps me with my sums."

"Oh, so that's why when I get home late, desperate for a cuppa and something to eat, you two have your heads together, bent over books. I always thought you were looking at comics or something."

They all knew Lou wasn't being altogether honest. She had always known that Eustace was smarter than she was. Sometimes she regretted her lack of schooling, wished she was more like Astrid, who was so smart she worked in a bookshop and was even going to be an author. Truly though, she really was happy with her lot. She was content to be just another factory girl, clocking in for her shift every morning and donning that horrible white cap on her hair to stop any stray bits from getting into the biscuit mixes. She liked the camaraderie of the factories. Bermondsey was full of them: Peek Freans, Sarson's Vinegar, and Hartley's Jam, which had moved into an old tannery. Then of course there was Pearce Duff's, which had moved into the old glue factory. They churned out loads of blancmange and custard powder each day.

Lou was quite happy at Peek Freans, even though she knew she could have probably earnt a few more shillings a week at one of the other factories.

At the same time though, she wanted better for her son. She didn't want him to end up like her, just factory fodder. He was a very smart, kind, gentle lad, and she had big ambitions for him.

"My manager at work gave me this book for you, Ben. Apparently it was given to his two boys, but they're not really readers. He remembered I'd said what a little bookworm you were, so he thought you might like it."

Ben was thrilled with the book: *Swallows and Amazons* by Arthur Ransome. It had only recently been published.

"Oh Mum, it's wonderful. I'll treasure it always. Can I have some paper to write him a thank-you note?"

"Of course you can, son. Have some of that nice fancy note paper your Aunty Astrid gave me for Christmas. By the way, I bet she's upset about two of her favourite authors dying this year, Arthur Conan Doyle and D.H. Lawrence. Bet they'll be a few happy readers up in heaven, though. The grandmas will be pleased to meet them on their fluffy clouds; they always enjoyed a good book."

"They'd both also be really glad about that new law, the Mental Treatment Act, I think it's being called. Apparently you'll be able to get free treatment if you go voluntarily to one of those new clinics, and they're not going to call them asylums any more. They're going to be called mental hospitals instead. Granny Ann would have been so happy to hear that if she was still alive; it always made her so sad when people talked about the asylums 'cos of her mum."

Eustace spoke up. "Life was so hard for women back then, especially if they was widowed young with a few kids to support. No wonder the old lady lost her mind."

"You're right, love, we women do have it a bit easier now. Look at that Amy Johnson, the first woman ever to fly solo all the way to Australia. Mind you, love, I would still like an inside bathroom!"

1933

I n 1933, everything changed for the Plant family.

There were big changes in the world, too.

Adolf Hitler had run in the 1932 elections. Although he was defeated, it soon became obvious that he had no intention of giving up his ideology. There was an Anti-Nazi Protest in London where thousands marched through the streets, waving placards objecting to the treatment of Jews in Germany.

The new Sydney Harbour Bridge had opened on the other side of the world, in Australia. One day, Ben intended to travel and see it for himself!

George Orwell had published a new book called *Down and Out in Paris and London,* which received reviews such as this:

"This is, in our view, an extremely forceful and socially important document."

But the most important - and most tragic - event in the life of the Plant family was the sudden death of Arthur Sr., husband to Jane and father to the six Plant girls.

Lou was distraught. As the youngest daughter, she had always felt a special bond with her dad. By the time she was born, the family had been a little more affluent, so there had been more time and money to indulge her a little more than her sisters. For example, when she started school, she had worn a brand-new pinafore dress with a shiny white ribbon tied in her hair. Her button boots had been second-hand, passed down through the family, but the leather on them was still good, thanks to her dad polishing them every night 'til they shone. She could picture all their shoes and boots lined up every night while her dad sat at the kitchen table, the table that had been covered in old newspapers to protect the wooden surface from getting ruined with lumps of black or brown boot polish. As a little girl she had watched, fascinated, while her big, strong father rolled up his shirtsleeves and carefully polished each shoe. She had always felt that he took extra care with hers, the tiniest of them all. Now, he would never polish another shoe.

"Oh Eustace, I'm going to miss him so much. He was the best dad in the world."

He kissed the top of her head gently as he held her firmly in his arms. She sobbed for what seemed like hours.

"Dad, aren't your arms aching? You've been cuddling Mum for ages."

He smiled sadly at his son. Luckily, he was too young yet to understand grief. While he had missed little Dennis greatly after he passed, Ben was too young to have truly acknowledged the unbearable pain of losing someone you loved so much.

"I'm all right, Ben. Your mum just needs us to take care of her right now. She's really upset about Granddad."

"I know, Dad. Me and Arthur are too. He said his mum has been crying all night. I know that's true, 'cos we could hear her through our bedroom wall."

Ben and his cousin Arthur Jr. shared a bedroom. They had done so all their lives, and they were as close as brothers - always looking out for each other.

"Can we go and see Granny Jane? She's been sitting out in the square all morning by herself. She looks so sad."

"Of course lad. You're good boys, she'll be happy to see you. Just don't wear her out with all your chat."

The two boys stopped in the rough patch of grass on the side of the square and picked a few daisies for their grandmother.

"Hello, Granny. We picked these to make you feel better."

The old lady lifted her head and smiled at them. They could tell she'd been crying, not in the noisy way that Arthur's mum had been, but quietly, on her own, out in the sunshine.

She was wearing black, "widow's weeds," they called them. She had never hated an outfit as much in her whole life. She clutched a white handkerchief in her wrinkled, old hand. It was soaking wet from all her tears.

"We're sad about Granddad, too. We loved him so much. He was the best granddad ever. He always played football with us and taught us the best way to roll our marbles so we always won."

"And he used to take us for long walks by the river and tell us stories of when he was young. He even took us right over the bridge sometimes, and showed us the Tower of London and St. Paul's. We would be so worn out when we got back that we'd pretend we were going to die unless he bought us ice creams."

The three of them fell quiet, each lost in their own memories of the old man.

Jane was bereft. The only man she had ever loved had been snatched away from her after 54 years together. It had been so sudden. One minute he was there, chatting away in his armchair in front of the fire, the next he had keeled over and dropped dead before her very eyes. Jane had been so shocked that she just sat there, holding his lifeless body in her arms and trying to will him back to life. Her beloved Arthur.

After a short time, she had run to the front door, screaming for help. Of course, it had been too late. Arthur was gone without even saying goodbye.

"When will we have to take Granddad to the cemetery? Will there be a glass carriage and horses like the two great-grannies had?"

The boys still remembered the splendid joint funeral.

They had been so proud to walk in the procession, even though they had heard some people muttering about them being too young. *"It's not right, them too little lads being made to go through that."* Arthur Jr. had turned 'round and stuck his tongue out at the two old women talking and Ben had laughed, wishing he was brave enough to do the same. They had both loved their great-grandmas dearly; they lived in the same house as them almost all their lives and it had been the boys themselves who insisted on being allowed to join the rest of the family as they walked beside the carriages.

"Oh, my little loves, we've got to do it tomorrow. I just don't know how I'm going to get through it. Your granddad has always been with me before. Every time I've been upset he has put those big strong arms around me and made everything alright. Now, he'll never be able to do that again."

She buried her head in her hands and wept quietly. The two boys comforted her as best they could, but were relieved when their mums came out and shooed them away.

Arthur Plant's funeral was just as grand as the one for the two old ladies had been. He was a much-loved and very well-respected man in his community. His family had lived and worked in Southwark for generations and he had never moved away, never wanted to venture further afield. The cobbled streets, old lanes and alleyways, and the River Thames had been his world - the only world he had ever desired.

Now, he was going to spend the rest of his days there, buried in the churchyard near the river in a plot next to his ancestors. His mum Mabel's grave was right next to his. They were the last Plants who would ever be buried there; the little churchyard was full. The old gravestones were so close together - as close as the people buried beneath them had been in life when they lived in the overcrowded tenements.

Sadly, Granny Ann and little Dennis had not been allowed to be interred in the bursting churchyard. After their funeral services in the old stone church, they had to be buried in the Nunhead Cemetery, a huge, rather forbidding place full of big, granite statues and marble angels. Everyone had especially been so sad to see the two old ladies, such good friends in life, be forced apart in death.

"At least Dad's work is close by so he can pop in and see granddad any time."

Lou tried not to sound cross as she spoke to her son. She wished she could just pop down the road every time she wanted to see her little Dennis. Now that she was working at the biscuit factory, it was sometimes a couple of weeks or more before she could get over to Nunhead Cemetery. But truthfully, it didn't matter. Her boy was always in her heart. She would never forget him, and at least the dreadful early days of her grief were behind her. She only had him in her life for two years and it had hurt so much to lose him. Her poor mum had been married for 54 wonderful years; she could not imagine the pain she must have been feeling.

Jane Plant went into something of a decline after losing her husband. She had always been a strong woman, but losing her mother, mother-in-law, and husband in such a short span of time was more than she could bear. She took to spending hours a day just sitting in front of the fire, staring into the orange flames. She forgot to eat and seemed to shrink before her family's very eyes.

"Lou, I've got something to tell you."

"Oh, don't tell me our Ben and Arthur have been up to mischief again?"

"No, no, it's nothing like that."

Ann sounded uncomfortable.

"Come on then, spit it out. I haven't got all day."

"Well, you know I've been seeing that bloke, Bob?"

It wasn't really a question; everyone in the Buildings had seen Bob collecting Ann to go dancing, then dropping her back home in his posh car.

"Yes."

"Well, he's asked me to marry him, and wants me and little Arthur to move to Whitstable."

She might as well have said Madagascar. The look on Lou's face said it all.

"Oh Ann, you're not really thinking of leaving London, are you? What about your job, what about all of us?"

She sounded close to tears. Her dad had just died, and now her big sister was talking about leaving her too.

"And... Bob's suggesting we take Mum with us. He knows how much I'd fret if I wasn't around to keep an eye on her."

Lou swallowed the remark that was about to fly out of her mouth - something about Ann not being the only one who looked out for their old mum. But she refrained, shut her mouth before the words were spoken.

"But Ann, I'd be so lonely with you gone. Our Amber is living the high life in Eastbourne, Astrid is preoccupied with her books, and the other two are so busy fighting with their horrible husbands that they wouldn't even notice if I was dead!"

"Oh Lou, you'll be fine. Whitstable isn't far! You can come and visit anytime you want. Plus, it will be good for your Ben to have holidays at the seaside."

Following Ann's bombshell of news, Lou started re-evaluating her life.

Although she had grown up in Peabody Buildings, maybe she didn't have to spend her whole life there after all. Her Eustace had been brave enough to see the world, maybe it was time she pulled up her socks and did something brave too.

"Eustace?"

"Yes, love?"

He didn't know why she always started the minute he got in from work. Sometimes, she didn't even wait for him to take off his jacket and boots. He quite liked it when she did a bit of overtime, then he could get home and relax a bit before she came inside.

"One of the girls at work is going out with a bloke who works for the council. He was telling her all about the slum clearances, and how they're building lots of council houses out in the country, to resettle people."

"Oh yes?"

"Well, I thought maybe we should apply, you know, for one of those new places. 'Course, it would mean leaving the Buildings, actually, getting out of London altogether."

She paused, waiting for his reaction.

Eustace was stunned. His wife was a Londoner, through and through. He had often heard her say that the only way she would ever leave Southwark was in a box.

"Oh, love. What's brought this on? I thought you were happy? Is it 'cos your dad's gone and Ann is threatening to move to Whitstable?"

"She's not just threatening it. Apparently, her Bob has inherited a house from his old aunty, which means they can move in straight away. They've even found a suitable place for young Arthur to do an apprenticeship. Apparently he fancies building boats, so I suppose it would be a good move for him too. You know how much he hated school. I'm amazed Ann managed to get him to stay there until he was fifteen. He hates working down at the market; he's been there for three years now and he moans all the time about what hard work it is. In that respect, he's more like his dad. I think. Although I do worry sometimes that he doesn't seem to be very interested in girls. Our Ann would love to be a grandma. Of course, he's not a clever clogs like our Ben is; even though he's so much older than our boy, he doesn't know half as much! Mind you, he doesn't have his head buried in a book all the time like our boy does.

Even Mum seems quite happy about the move. She told me today that after going to visit Amber a few times down in Eastbourne, she quite fancied living by the seaside herself. Apparently they have great oysters and whelks down in Whitstable, and you know how she's always loved those. Bob's sold her on the idea by saying that his house is right on the seafront, so she can walk on the beach every day, summer or winter."

Lou sounded a bit forlorn, and it broke his heart. He had not seen her so upset since that awful time after their Dennis died. Now, she seemed to feel that she was going to lose the rest of her family in one fell swoop.

"Even Astrid says she might think about moving down that way too, when she retires. Says that living by the sea will be good for her writing!"

Eustace, having listened patiently, took a few minutes to gather his thoughts before he replied.

"But our boy is happy at his school. Do you really think it's fair to uproot him, to take him away from everything he knows?"

Really, Eustace was talking about himself. Was he ready to be uprooted, taken away from everything and everyone he had ever known?

A NEW LIFE

They left Southwark on a bright, sunny day in 1934.

It took a while for Lou to convince Eustace that it was the right move for their family, but in the end, she won.

Despite his reticence, he had finally been beaten down by her sadness, as her whole family seemed to disappear before her very eyes.

First the two grannies, then her dad, and now Ann, their mum Jane, and little Arthur. They had all gone, some to their graves and some to Whitstable, a pretty little seaside town on the Kent coast. It was truly not that far away as the crow flies, but far enough that, to a heartbroken Lou, it seemed like they had disappeared to Africa.

Of course they had gone to Whitstable for a visit - had spent two lovely weekends there - but somehow, that only made it worse. It hurt Lou to see her sister starting a new life, away from the grime and misery of the city. A healthy, outdoorsy kind of life, where the air was clean and you could see the ocean. And the oysters... Well, they were certainly to die for!

On their visit, Lou saw that her family all looked so happy and healthy. Ann and their mum had put on a few pounds, which really suited them. Gone was that pale, pinched look that so many women from Southwark seemed to have. Instead, their cheeks were rosy and they seemed to smile much more.

Young Arthur had an apprenticeship with the local boat builder, so he was in seventh heaven. He took Ben on a tour of the boatyard, pointing out all the new things he was learning.

Ben was enthralled. He had always loved his cousin, but now his cousin seemed like a man - no longer just a big boy. He was proud of his big cousin, who had happily played football and marbles with him, whom he had shared a bedroom with all his life.

He hardly recognised this new Arthur. He seemed to have grown since they left London. Like his mum and grandma, he had put on a bit of weight. He had muscles, his cheeks were ruddy from working outside all day, and he seemed to have so much more energy and enthusiasm for life.

"I reckon you ought to persuade your mum and dad to come down here. You'd really like living here, Ben. Just think of all the fun we'd have. It'd be just like old times."

They were walking along the pebbly beach, idly picking up the odd flat stone and skipping it across the water.

"If you lot stay in Southwark, you might end up working at the market like I did. Or worse still, slog your guts out at the docks like your dad has to."

Ben was quiet. He knew that his mum and dad had big plans for him. They didn't want him to just end up in some run-of-the-mill job at the docks; they wanted him to get a good education and make something of himself.

Anyway, finally, the decision was made. They would not be going to Whitstable sadly, but instead, moving out to the country.

"Oh come on Eustace, it's not that far - less than 15 miles from here. You'll be able to get the Tube from Morden right through to London Bridge in just half an hour or so. Then you can easily walk to the docks."

She was so enthusiastic.

"But Lou, that means I'll have to leave home at five o'clock in the morning to get to work on time. And how am I going to get to the Underground at Morden? I s'pose you expect me to walk there as well?"

"Don't be silly, love. I've checked, and there's a bus that goes from the top of our road right to the Tube station. It'll only take about ten minutes."

He tried to resist for a couple of weeks, but in the end, she wore him down. For the love of his wife, he agreed to alter his whole life. He was agreeing to leave the place where he had grown up - the only home he had ever known (well, apart from those few years at sea) - and embark on a whole new life in the country.

The day after she had heard about all the new council houses being built, Lou left work early and went to the council offices. She had to queue for ages; obviously word had got out and she wasn't the only one who wanted a new start for her family.

It had taken a few months to get onto the list. Lou and Eustace had had visits from various council officials in order to check that the information on their application form was correct - that they did indeed live in a rather old, shabby flat with no running water or toilet.

Lou had to show the rather snooty official around the Buildings' big laundry room, the communal bath house, and the toilet block, which was used by the whole square. He seemed shocked, particularly when she told him about all the poverty and disease they experienced.

"But you know, Eustace, the *funniest* thing was when I took him out to the washing lines in the square. It was Monday, so the lines were full and there were a couple of girls still pegging out their sheets. He asked me how much of our washing got stolen, hanging out there altogether in the sunshine. When I told him nothing ever went missing, except maybe if a kid decided to pinch a sheet to make a tent, he was so surprised. I said to him, 'We *might be poor, but we are all honest'*; that seemed to shut him up. I suppose blokes like him live in fancy houses and don't know the half of how most people live."

She paused for breath.

"Anyway, he reckoned we've got a good case and should hear very soon."

They heard within a fortnight that they had been allocated a brand new house on a new council estate, in a place called Rosehill.

"Where's Rosehill, Mum? Will I like it there? What about my school?"

"I know Rosehill. It's that little place after Morden, before you get to Sutton. You must remember, Lou, we used to go through it on the charabanc on our way to the Derby."

Every year, the dockers organised a day trip to Epsom Downs to watch the Derby. They took a picnic, sat on the grass with all the other thousands of day-trippers, and the men had a little flutter on the horses.

"Oh yes, I remember it now. I can't quite picture it, mind you, but won't it be grand to live so near the racecourse? We'll probably be able to just get a bus there."

In truth, now that it was becoming more than just a pipe dream, Lou was also getting anxious about the move. Despite all her big talk, she was a Londoner through and through. She spoke like a Cockney and felt at home amongst her own kind in Southwark, but this was an opportunity. It was a chance for them to make something of themselves.

"I hope you've started thinking about what you're going to grow in our new garden, Eustace. Ben and I are expecting some giant vegetables, aren't we, son? And I wouldn't mind you growing me a few nice flowers. I could pick them and put them on the mantelpiece in Granny Ann's old vase."

When the day came to leave Peabody Buildings, they were all in tears. Astrid took the day off work to come down and help them pack. She was going to spend a few days in the new house helping Lou get settled in while Eustace was at work. Ben was looking forward to a couple of weeks off to get to know his new surroundings, and hopefully make some new friends before he started at the grammar school. He had just passed the entrance exams for it. He was a very smart boy, so they were welcoming him with open arms.

The sun shone as the little family piled their few possessions into a little van. Eustace had been lucky enough to borrow it from work, on the understanding that they could use it from 8am until midday, when it needed to be back at the docks.

There wasn't much to pack. The old pine kitchen table and four chairs, a couple of worn old armchairs, their beds, a few pots and pans, and their clothes. Ben had a separate box for his few toys and books.

All their neighbours came out to say goodbye.

Eustace's workmate from the docks, who was going to drive the van, stood by impatiently as one person after another embraced and gave the family a small token to remember them by: a lace hanky, a box of toffees, a new fountain pen for Ben.

Lou thought Peabody Buildings had never looked so good, so inviting. Its old brick façade was splendid in the bright morning sun.

"Bye, bye, see you all soon! You must come down and visit us; we've got plenty of room. We'll miss you."

Lou was a soggy mess by the time the van reached the outskirts of the city. Suddenly it hit her: Wishing for a bright, new future meant leaving behind everything she had ever known. Stepping into this new life suddenly seemed quite scary!

Astrid squeezed her hand. The two women were sitting in the back seat while Ben and his dad were perched up front, chatting away to the driver.

"It'll be alright, Lou. I think you're doing the right thing. You could have spent your whole life in Southwark, never realising what a big, exciting world was waiting for you out there. This way, you'll never have any regrets about not trying something different. I've bought a big pile of books to leave with you, in case you get lonely in your big, new house while your Ben is at school and Eustace is at work."

They all gasped when the van drew up outside the house on Garendon Road. They hadn't seen it yet, hadn't even seen an artist's impression of what it would be like, so it was a very pleasant surprise.

The house was a brand-new, brick-built house in a row of ten, but theirs was the corner house. Instead of having their "front door" at the front like all the others, it was at the side, with a little canopy to protect it from the elements. There was a small garden at the front and a low brick wall surrounding the property, giving an air of privacy from their neighbours.

While Lou was fumbling in her handbag for the key, Eustace and Ben disappeared through the tall wooden gate at the side.

"Mum, Mum! Aunty Astrid! Come quick."

As they walked through the gateway into the back garden, the first things Lou noticed were the silly grins on the faces of her husband and son.

"Look, Mum. There's enough room to play football! And Dad says we can grow potatoes, carrots, cabbages, maybe even a bit of fruit. I'd love a big tree that I could climb."

Both Lou and Astrid were in tears looking at the little garden. It wasn't huge, but it was certainly big enough to grow a bit in. And they had their own washing line!

Eventually they dragged themselves out of the garden, only because the van driver kept making noises: *"Don't forget, I've got to get back to Southwark this week!"* In reality, he was a bit envious; how he wished he could get his family a nice place like this. Maybe he'd go to the council tomorrow and put their name on the list. Mind you, his missus wasn't as brave as that Lou; he was not sure he'd manage to drag her out of Bermondsey.

The inside of the house was just as good as the garden. You walked straight from the front door into a tiny little hallway, where a flight of stairs took up almost all the room. There was a little cupboard underneath the stairs to store coal for the fire, and another one for shoes, toys, or whatever the new owners might fancy. Then, you walked into a smallish lounge that had an open fireplace with a tiled mantelpiece.

There was the kitchen, a reasonably-sized room big enough to hold their old table and chairs. It had a big stone butler's sink and a fancy little boiler on the wall above it to heat the hot water. As if this wasn't enough luxury, there was a door off the kitchen which led to a small bathroom. In the bathroom was a bath and a hand basin.

"Where's the toilet, Mum? Is it outside?

Eustace beamed and flung open another door. Like the rest of the house, the walls inside were painted in shades of brown, cream, and green. In the centre of the room, in pride of place, sat a brand-new white toilet.

To a family who, until that moment, had to share toilet facilities with lots of other families - sometimes as many as twenty or thirty people - this was luxury indeed. And it was inside! There would be no more trudging across a cold, dark square or managing with a pot under the bed. None of them could keep the smiles from their faces.

Upstairs there were two bedrooms. The bigger one was at the front of the house, overlooking the street, and they put Lou and Eustace's big feather bed in there. It was a splendid thing made of brass, with fancy, twirly ends that were a devil to dust. Eustace had got it cheap from a bloke at the docks, an accountant or something, whose wife had run off with a sailor. She had broken his heart in leaving, so he wanted to sell their marital bed. Eustace hadn't told Lou he had bought it, just surprised her one day by getting it delivered while he was at work. He had been in her good books for weeks after that!

The back bedroom overlooked the garden. Ben thought he might die of excitement. Excitement at having his own room in this beautiful new house with a garden view out the window. He had seen lots of big green spaces just around the corner; he and his new mates could play football in those so they didn't spoil anyone's new veg plants.

"Well, what do you think Ben? Do you reckon you'll like living in the country?"

His Aunty Astrid had come into the room. She was his favourite aunty in the world. The others were alright, of course, but there was something special about Aunty Astrid. He wondered if it was because she had no husband or kids of her own, or whether it was because she was interesting and loved books so much. Whatever it was, he adored her and loved to spend hours just sitting quietly beside her while they were both absorbed in their latest read.

"I'm so glad you're staying with us, Aunty Astrid. There's plenty of room in here for both of us. Dad says he'll buy me a bookshelf to go in that corner, and maybe a chest of drawers or a wardrobe for my clothes."

To little Ben, the bookshelf idea was far more desirable than somewhere to put his clothes.

"Anyway, Dad got a camp-bed from a bloke down the market so that we'd have somewhere for visitors to sleep. I'll have that tonight and you can have my bed."

When the clock on the mantelpiece struck two o'clock, they were more or less settled in. All the beds were made, the pots and pans were in the kitchen cupboard, and everyone was relaxing in the living room - the *front room*, as Lou insisted on calling it.

"We don't want to start getting no airs and graces just 'cos we've moved into a posh house. We're the same people we've always been, still Londoners, through and through."

"I think we should go for a bit of a stroll. See what this new place has to offer."

Eustace held the door open as his family all trooped out. He gave his wife a big grin as she passed him, and she grinned back at him as she commented.

"Well thank-you, kind sir. Nice of you to let us visit your posh palace!"

They were all in good spirits as they wandered around the streets. A few of the houses had tenants already, but some of them were still empty, waiting to be finished.

"I reckon we've got one of the best ones, don't you? 'Cos our house is a corner one, it seems a bit more exclusive somehow. And our garden's bigger."

They admired all the big, green spaces on the estate that were planned especially for children to run around and play football or cricket. They passed a new block of flats, very smart, art deco style ones, which were painted bright white.

"I'm glad they didn't give us one of those... Would have felt a bit too much like old Peabody Buildings."

"But at least they've probably got their own toilets, like us."

They walked right up to the main road, the London to Brighton road. It was busy with buses, carriages, and the odd car or van, so it took them a while to cross the wide street.

"Look at that smashing building over there, Dad! It looks like an ocean liner. And there's shops underneath it."

Eustace was busy looking at the big public house, The Rose. Maybe that was somewhere he could pop into occasionally; it would be good to meet some new mates over a pint or two.

Lou had gone very quiet.

"Look, you lot. Can you believe it? Our very own cinema."

She was pointing to a large, white building. Alongside the little shops, the tobacconist's, the newsagent, and the greengrocers, was another building. The Gaumont.

Her husband could see the tears in her eyes.

"Oh love, I never thought it was going to be as nice as this. There's so much. All them shops, everything we could possibly need, and now there's a cinema, too. I reckon I've died and gone to heaven."

Lou had always loved the cinema. When they were courting, she made Eustace take her once a week, twice sometimes if he was feeling a bit flush.

"Now I'll be able to just pop up the road and go whenever I like."

They all smiled at her enthusiasm.

"And how exactly are you proposing to pay for all these little jaunts, my girl? We'll have extra expenses with Ben's new school uniform and my fares to work. Now that you've given up your job to become queen of the castle, I'm not sure how we're going to manage."

She punched his arm playfully.

"I just want to get us all settled, get Ben into the new school, then I'll start looking around for something. I bet there's a few places 'round here that would love to take on someone with my experience and charm!"

"Look Mum, there's even a Woolworths. I could pop in there every Saturday to spend my pocket money."

By the time they got home, they were worn out. It had been a busy, emotional day and they were all glad to get to bed that night, even though truthfully, none of them slept very well. It was too quiet and too dark. There were no carriages rolling along cobbled streets, no drunkards falling out of the pubs at closing time, no gas lights lighting up the dark, gloomy alleyways. Just a clear, dark sky filled with twinkling stars.

The little family was awakened early the next morning by the sound of the milkman in his electric cart, glass milk bottles clattering in the steel crates.

Eustace leapt out of bed, threw on his trousers, and rushed out of the front door. He came back beaming, holding two glass bottles full of the white stuff.

"Okay, love. That's all sorted. He'll drop off two bottles every day, one gold top and one red one. He says he usually gets here by nine o'clock, but if we're not home, he'll tuck it 'round the corner by the back gate 'cos it's a bit cooler there. Won't matter in the winter of course, it'll keep nice and cold then, but we don't want it curdling on hot days before we get the chance to drink it.

We don't have to pay him till Saturday and we can change the order anytime we like, just have to give him a couple of days' notice. He said not to worry if the tops have little holes in them, it's just where the birds try to steal the cream!"

Despite all these little luxuries - the garden, the inside toilet, her own washing line, and the milk deliveries - Lou pined. She pined for Southwark, for her old life, the only life she had ever known. She missed her workmates at the factory, her friends, Borough Market, the River Thames. She realised how much she had taken those things for granted. Moving away allowed her to see them in a new light.

At the same time though, she loved her new surroundings. Her family was thriving in Sutton.

Ben had started at the grammar school and loved it. He had already made some new friends and a few of them lived on the same estate. Every evening, one could find them outside together playing football.

Lou had started to make friends, too. Gradually, the surrounding houses started to fill with tenants - mostly young families from London like them. Some were nice, the kind of people you would want to spend time with. Others were the sort you nodded to politely in the street, but never invited into your home for a cup of tea.

As suspected, Eustace was the one who struggled the most with the move. His life had changed beyond recognition.

Instead of just walking 'round the corner to the docks, he had to wake up at four o'clock, get washed and dressed, have a quick cuppa, then run to catch the bus. The bus took him to Morden, where he then had to catch the Tube to London Bridge. The commute added another three hours to each working day - one and a half hours in the morning and another one and a half hours to get back at night. Although he hated it and missed his life in London, it was worth it, too. Worth it to see his Lou looking so happy.

The next few years were pretty good ones for the family. Eustace eventually got used to the long commute and even began to enjoy it, spending the journey in both directions with his head in the newspaper.

Ben flourished; he loved his new school, loved his new friends, and loved being outside in the clean, fresh air - either playing football with his mates or helping his dad in the garden. He joined the local Boys' Brigade and even enjoyed going to the church group attached to it. It was a bit like a big boys' Sunday school.

Over time, Lou got herself a job at the local seed factory.

She loved being back in the old factory atmosphere, laughing and joking with all her new-found friends. It was much easier work than the biscuit factory had been. She was never too tired to come home from work and cook a nice, nutritious meal for her boys. Everyone settled into a comfortable pattern, a new lifestyle that suited them all - a million light years away from their old life in the slums.

They ate fresh vegetables from their own garden every day. Grandma Ann's precious old vase on the mantelpiece was always filled with something pretty: a few colourful dahlias, daffodils in the spring, or a bunch of wild bluebells Ben would pick in the woods for his mum.

They bought a big copper boiler and an old-fashioned wringer. The boiler was in the corner of the kitchen, ready for the Monday morning wash before Lou headed off to the factory. All the women were a bit weary when they got to work on Mondays, having got up at the crack of dawn to: put the dirty stuff in the boiler, put it through the wringer outside the back door, and peg it out on the line in the garden.

Despite being tired, Lou didn't mind doing this house-work. It was wonderful that she could do the washing in her own home instead of spending all that time in the communal laundry. Plus, she loved seeing her two boys go out the door each day looking smart in their clean, starched white shirts and collars.

"Mum. Why do you have to do the washing every Monday? Why can't you do it on Tuesday, Wednesday, or even Thursday? I don't understand."

Lou put down the darning she was holding. She seemed to have a big pile to do every evening. Her husband and son were forever making holes in their socks, and Ben's shorts appeared to develop new splits and tears every other day.

"And why's that thing called a *mushroom*? Silly name if you ask me. You can't even eat it, it's just an old piece of wood!"

She looked down at the darning on the table beside her.

"You're right, son. I don't know why they call it a mush-room. It is a bit of a silly name, but it's a good shape to fit your socks while I mend them. I just don't know how you and your dad manage to make so many holes in them. I'd have much more time to laze around in the evenings if it weren't for you two giving me all this extra work!"

"But *why* do you have to wash every Monday? I don't understand. Surely the clothes would get just as clean on another day during the week?"

She looked across at her son, lounging in his father's armchair. Eustace wasn't home from work yet, so Ben was making the most of sitting in his chair in his absence.

"Oh, love, I don't really know why. It's just what we've always done. My mum did it, both grandmas did it, and probably everyone did it for hundreds of years before that. It's just tradition, I suppose. A bit like eating fish on Fridays."

"By the way, Ben, the factory is organising a charabanc trip to Brighton next month. Do you fancy coming with us?"

She knew the answer before he even opened his mouth to reply.

"Oh Mum, I'm almost sixteen now. Why would you think I'd want to go on a coach trip with a load of old people? I'd much rather stay here and play football with my mates. I can always go to Sid's house for my tea; his mum likes having me 'round. Says I've got a good appetite, and she's a really good cook."

Lou bristled slightly. It was hard when your child - your only child - would clearly rather spend time with his mate's family than spend time with his own.

"Mum, please don't get upset. You know I love your cooking and I love spending time with you and Dad. I just don't want to sit on a bus for hours with a whole load of old cronies, whose idea of 'fun' is stopping at every pub en route and singing old Cockney tunes all the way home."

His mother winced. Ben had described the trip to a tee. Sometimes she worried that he was becoming a bit of a snob, not liking all the things he had once been so fond of. When he was a little lad, he loved belting out the old songs. You could find him standing on a chair while someone played the piano to "Roll Out the Barrel," or "The Lambeth Walk," or "There'll always be an England."

Now, she supposed, he had become a Surrey boy - more fond of classical music than the old music hall songs. Lou sometimes felt a bit uncomfortable when they went to things at that grammar school of his. Most of the other parents weren't Londoners like she and Eustace were. They were different; they spoke with a bit of a plum in their mouth and she always felt they rather looked down on her and her docker husband.

But Ben loved the school, and if the price they had to pay for his happiness was him turning his back on his origins, then so be it. One day, when he was grown, he would realise the value of family connections.

The family popped over to Whitstable a couple of times a year to see Ann and her family. Young Arthur was now a fully-fledged boatbuilder and still worked at the little boatyard by the seafront. He was dating the boss's daughter, and everyone expected them to marry within the year. She was a nice girl - quiet, with no airs and graces - and she treated Ann and Grandma Jane with respect.

Astrid was still living in London, and it seemed she likely wouldn't be moving to Whitstable when she retired, after all. The old lady she lived with had died, and in her will, she had bequeathed everything to Astrid - provided she stayed in the house and took care of the four cats. Although the only unwed Plant daughter loved her London life, seeing her three sisters thrive in other places - Ann in Whitstable, Amber in Eastbourne, and Lou in Rosehill - often left her wondering if staying in the city had been the right decision. Sometimes, she even wondered if she had missed out by not having a husband and a couple of kids. However, that ship had sailed; it was too late to wonder about all that now. Plus, there were far bigger fish to fry.

It was 1938, and the world seemed to be in a rather precarious state. A lot of the old academics who came into Astrid's bookshop seemed convinced that there would soon be another war.

"Now that Hitler has marched into Austria, there's much worse to come, trust me."

"Have you heard what his thugs have been up to? They're calling it *Kristallnacht*. All those poor Jews whose shops, homes, and synagogues have been destroyed. And they reckon they're shipping thousands of them off to special camps."

The following year, their words rang true. On the 1st September 1939, Germany invaded Poland. Two days later, Great Britain and France declared war on Germany. The Second World War had begun.

THE WAR YEARS: 1939-1945

O nce war was declared, Lou was glad she was out of London. In Sutton they were out of the thick of it, away from Hitler's bombs and all the sadness and carnage on the streets.

Truthfully, the year had started out so well.

The king and queen had gone to America to meet with the president. There had been lots of handshaking and fine words spoken. The royal couple returned to England in a blaze of glory. Bands greeted their arrival home, there were flags and bunting everywhere, and the two young princesses, Elizabeth and Margaret, welcomed their parents home as the band played "Land of Hope and Glory."

At first, just like the last time, everyone thought the war would be over quickly.

Eustace wouldn't be called up to fight this time around; besides the fact that he had not miraculously grown since being rejected in 1914, he was now too old to fight. In addition, his job on the docks was still considered essential work, necessary to the war effort.

Ben, thank goodness, was not yet of age to be called up. He was only sixteen, still in school. He was no longer at the grammar school, but was studying electronics engineering at the local technical college. He was so smart and very hard-working. He had even signed up for some extra evening classes so he could get a few more certificates to help him when he eventually started looking for a job.

Everyone was hopeful the war wouldn't last. Lou was sure it would be over before her boy turned eighteen.

Ann was relieved that her son, Arthur, although much older than Ben, was deemed exempt from fighting due to his boat building skills. He was a gentle boy, totally unsuited to fire a rifle at some unseen enemy. Luckily, the owner of the boatyard had friends in high places, and he had no intention of letting his new son-in-law get sent off to fight in what he considered to be a senseless war. Besides, Arthur's wife was due to give birth to twins soon, and her father refused to allow his precious girl to become a widow.

All across the country, mothers were losing their sons to yet another futile war.

Children were being evacuated out of London to the relative safety of the country. Lou's heart went out to all their mothers; she couldn't imagine the heartbreaking feeling of waving your kids off at the train station, watching them pull away with little gas masks and their suitcases in hand. These mothers said good-bye to their precious little ones, not knowing when - or if - they would see them again.

Everyone was issued a gas mask. They were supposed to take them everywhere they went, but sometimes, Lou purposely left hers on the kitchen table.

"I'll be damned if I'm going to let that little squirt Hitler tell me what to do! Our boys will finish him and his lot off by Christmas."

But she was wrong. By Christmas, the situation was only worse. Men and boys were being enlisted and there were sandbags and blackouts everywhere. Men were volunteering for organisations like Civil Defence and the Home Guard. They had even built a large public air raid shelter out of brick on Green Lane, just around the corner from Lou and Eustace's house. The war was certainly creeping closer to their little world.

"I've signed up for the Home Guard, Lou."

"Oh Eustace, did you have to? Don't you think you're a bit old for all that malarkey? The docks will be a prime target, you know. Old Hitler will be sure to bomb those as hard as he can. I wish you'd just quit and stay home with me and Ben. You could retire now, you know. We'd manage. We've got my bit coming in from the factory and you could easily get a nice little job down here - away from London. I worry about you every time you leave the house, thinking it might be the last time I see you."

She burst into tears and he crossed the room to take her in his arms. Even after all these years - after 27 years of marriage - they still adored each other.

"Sorry, Lou. I can't just sit back while all these young men go off to war. I don't want to be one of those blokes who hides away behind his wife's apron."

"I bet Amber's Fred is going to make a pretty packet this time 'round. He did well enough in the last war; this time it'll be much easier for him to deal in the black market."

Neither of them had any time for Amber's husband, but they had to tolerate him. Amber had committed to staying with him long ago, even though she knew about his illegal business dealings and illicit affairs. She decided she would rather live with all that - in the luxury he could provide for her and her daughters - than risk being alone with no income or no social standing.

"We fight on, for King and Empire, for Freedom."

Eustace was angry. They had just come out of the cinema, having watched the Pathé newsreel - the Review of the Year (1939). He took a bite of the chip Lou offered him.

It had become a bit of a routine since they moved to Rosehill - they went to the pictures on Saturday nights, then walked home eating fish and chips from the wrapper. Usually it was one of his favourite activities, but tonight, he was rattled.

"All those young men. So many brave souls, dying. And for what? It's just as much of a bloody farce as it was last time. Back in 1914 we were all told we were 'fighting for freedom,' ensuring world peace. The 'war to end all wars.'"

They had both cried during the newsreel. It was like watching history repeat itself.

Their house was in darkness when they got home. Obviously, Ben was still 'round at his friend Sid's house. He seemed to spend all his spare time there lately. Both boys were studying at the technical college. Sid was just as bright as Ben, that's probably why they were such firm friends.

When Ben did get home, he seemed to bring the cold in with him. It was October 1940 now, and the evenings were getting chillier.

"Hello, Mum, hello, Dad. I think you'd better sit down."

Lou's heart sank. Surely, he wasn't going to say he'd joined up.

"Sid and I went down to the recruiting office today."

"Oh, Ben."

"Don't fuss, Mum. Don't be as bad as Sid's mum was. We called into their place first and she had a fit - weeping and wailing all over the place. Said she 'didn't give birth to him just to see him returned to her in a coffin.' I'm glad you're not that dramatic. Sid was still trying to calm her down when I left."

"Oh son. You're so young. Only just 18, too young to go to war."

"Don't be silly, Dad. We saw boys down there who I know for a fact are younger than me. No one seemed to care much that they were lying about their age to get in. At least Sid and I are old enough to fight. Anyway, it's done now. We've signed up for the Air Force; we both fancy flying planes. They reckon we'll get our call-up papers in a few weeks, then we'll be sent off for training."

He sounded so excited. His parents' hearts were silently breaking at the thought of their precious boy going off to war, but they didn't want to be like Sid's mum - dramatic, *"weeping and wailing all over the place."*

That night, in their big feather bed, Eustace held Lou tightly while she cried in a way he hadn't seen her do since they lost their little Dennis, all those years ago.

The two boys got their call-up papers and their smart Royal Air Force (RAF) uniforms a few months later, then they set off for training. Unfortunately, they found a few small health issues that disqualified Ben from being able to fly planes, but Sid passed each examination with flying colours.

"I'm disappointed, of course I am. I was really looking forward to learning to fly a plane, but they offered me something else instead. They were very impressed with my electronic engineering background and they know I'm good at maths, so they're going to send me to South Africa."

"South Africa!"

"Yes. Isn't it exciting? I've always wanted to go abroad. Apparently it's really hot out there; we'll have to wear tropical uniforms and everything."

"But what will you do in South Africa? I didn't think there was any fighting there."

"No, Mum, there isn't at the moment. But they do maintenance out there; it'll be my job to keep all the planes well maintained so they stay up in the air. I'll be checking all the propellers and wheels and stuff."

He didn't mention that part of his job might also include putting bombs and bullets into the planes. He could tell his mum was worried enough already.

Ben and Sid set off after training, two bright-eyed and bushy-tailed young men going off to do their bit for King and Country. Heading toward foreign lands for a bit of adventure.

Sadly, Sid would never come back. On his third mission, his plane was shot down and the whole crew perished. His body was later recovered - along with the bodies of his crewmates. They were all completely unrecognisable, having been burnt to death by enemy fire.

Ben, on the other hand, had a lovely war. He loved the sunshine, the palm trees, and the people of South Africa. He flourished under the hot, African sun and became extremely popular, both for his sunny personality and his excellent skills at mending aircraft. Although he was naturally a quiet boy, once he got talking it was hard to stop him. He was so passionate, enthusiastic, and kind.

Several of the local girls and a few daughters of the RAF officers who were permanently stationed there took a real liking to the young Englishman. Although he was unfailingly polite, he never returned the advances. He much preferred the camaraderie of the airfield and the dining mess with his mates. They became a tight little unit, all watching out for each other and mourning when yet another plane was shot down. Mourning as more young men were declared gone forever.

Ben was sent to several different places: Johannesburg, Cape Town, Durban, Port Elizabeth, and East London. That last one made him smile, *East London*, it was nothing like the East London he knew back in Old Blighty.

He wrote postcards and sent a few of them back to his mum and dad, but was never sure if they would receive them. The old censors were a bit too trigger happy with their thick black pens, erasing anything that could be considered a threat to the war effort. He could understand them not wanting the folks back home to hear about any of the awful atrocities happening on the front lines - the news about men and boys being senselessly killed. However, blokes like him who were just enjoying all that beautiful South Africa had to offer? Surely, men like him were no threat at all. In fact, it would probably lift everyone's spirits to hear about the glorious beaches, constant sunshine, palm trees, and pineapples. Ben had been hoping to see a few wild animals while stationed down there, but so far, they had been too busy for that.

Day after day, he and his crewmates had to mend the planes that limped back to the airfields after battle. Sometimes the planes were so damaged, it was hard to believe the crews who were inside of them got out alive.

The planes were patched up as best they could be, the men in South Africa making sure they were airworthy before loading them with bombs and bullets and readying them for the next night's raids. Everyone was hoping against hope that the crews manning the bandaged aircraft would return in one piece.

On their days off, they roamed around, enjoying the sunshine and the kindness of the locals and trying out new foods - unusual things like pineapples, which they had never seen before. Ben took a liking to all the currys on offer - again something he had never experienced back in England. He didn't care whether they contained goat, fish, or whatever, he just loved the tanginess, the rather exotic taste.

Like Ben, many of the RAF service members in South Africa were very young and handsome, so it was no surprise that they attracted attention wherever they went. Somehow, RAF personnel had acquired the nickname, "the Brylcreem Boys," and the nice-looking men certainly lived up to that description. With their good looks, fit bodies, and newly-tanned skin, they looked as good as any model on a poster advertising the famous hair cream.

Ben was surprised to see photographers on the streets in South Africa, just as there had been back in London. These people offered to take a photo for a few shillings. As they said, *"A souvenir to send home to your mothers, to show them what their handsome young boys are up to."*

Ben got a couple of these photos and sent them home. There was one of him strolling along the street in Johannesburg, wearing his smart RAF uniform. Another, just a head and shoulders photo, was taken in a little studio in Cape Town. He popped them inside a Christmas card, across the front of both of them writing: *"To the best parents in the world. Love, Ben."*

Lou cried for days when she finally received her son's card with the two photos tucked inside. She didn't get it until July 1943, two years after her boy had gone away. Up till then, she had just received a few of the official letters servicemen were allowed to send - brief, uninformative little scraps of paper with any potentially sensitive information indecipherable, due to the censor's pen. She knew her boy had arrived safely at his destination and that he was still in one piece, but apart from that, she knew almost nothing.

Every day she thanked God that Ben's health issues had stopped him from flying unlike his poor friend, Sid. God rest his soul. She had seen his mother in the street a few times since having heard the news of his passing. She looked awful; even though she had previously been quite a big woman, she now looked like a bag of bones. And her eyes... Lou couldn't bear to think about the pain that poor woman was going through. Not only had she lost her Sid, but his two younger brothers were fighting too - one in the Army and the other in the Navy. Every day, Lou imagined the poor woman lived in dread of a telegram arriving, telling her the worst. She had just one daughter left at home now, a pretty girl, about the same age as their Dennis would have been. Doreen, her name was. According to the gossip on the street - which Lou tried to avoid listening to... mostly - Doreen had been gallivanting around with a Yank, a young airman. Now that she was pregnant with his baby, it turned out he already had a wife and three little kiddies back in Ohio.

The baby must be due any day now; Lou had seen Doreen in Woolworths recently buying some baby clothes.

"Hello, love, how are you?"

"Oh, I'm okay, thanks."

"How's your mum? I was so sad to hear about your Sid. Ben was so upset at the news; he and Sid were like brothers. Always in each other's pockets."

The girl broke down in tears, right there in the middle of the shop. Doreen was sobbing quietly, her enormous tummy under the voluminous smock, heaving up and down with every cry.

"Let's go and have a nice cup of tea, love. It might make you feel a bit better. My feet are killing me, so I could do with a nice sit down."

Lou had been on her feet all day at the factory and had just popped into the shops to buy something for Eustace's tea.

They sat in a window seat of the little café. It was a bit more private there.

Doreen recovered a bit. "I'm sorry. I didn't mean to make a fuss back there. It's all just such a mess. Mum's in pieces about our Sid and worried to death about the other boys. Now I've just added to her worries... Fine daughter I turned out to be."

Lou's heart went out to the distraught girl in front of her. She was so young, only about sixteen or seventeen.

"Do you want to talk about it, love? The baby, I mean."

"I never wanted a baby. I just wanted a bit of fun. I pretended to be older and went to the dance hall with my friend and her sisters - they're all nineteen or twenty and looking for husbands. We met these Yanks. They were really nice to us, gave us chocolate and silk stockings. We saw them a few times at the dance hall, then one of them, Jerry was his name, asked me to go to the pictures with him. We went to The Rose for a drink afterwards. I sat outside in the beer garden, 'cos they know my mum and dad in there and I didn't want them to know I was drinking. I only had a couple of drinks, but it went to my head a bit. He walked me home along Love Lane and made some joke about being in a romantic mood. Next thing I know, we're behind the bushes."

She took a big gulp of tea before continuing.

"I saw him a few more times after that and the night always ended the same, going behind the bushes on the way home. Then I realised I was pregnant. I didn't mind; I thought he would marry me and I could be one of those war brides who goes off to start a new life in America. When I told him the news, he went a bit pale. Admitted he already had a wife and three little kiddies back home. Now he's gone off to war and I don't suppose he'll ever see this baby."

She began sobbing again and people started to stare.

"Look love, let's finish our tea and we'll walk home together. I just need to pop into the fishmonger's first to get some kippers for my husband's tea... If they've got any left, that is."

Food had been in short supply as the war continued to drag on. Everyone was losing weight, either through worry, lack of nutrition, or both. It was such a hard time for so many people.

London had suffered greatly. German bombs had destroyed so much of the city. Everywhere you looked, there was devastation.

Eustace had to spend some nights in town guarding the docks, so occasionally Lou went up there to join him. She would either stay at an old friend's in Peabody Buildings or with Astrid at her little house in Chelsea.

She was more horrified by the city every time she went. With each visit, the London she knew and loved seemed to disappear before her very eyes. She often wandered to Bermondsey, taking the route she had used so many times before on her way to work at the biscuit factory. There was desolation everywhere.

St. John's Church in Bermondsey - better known as the *Louse* church because of its fancy steeple - was damaged by an incendiary bomb. Because of that, many houses in the city were destroyed. Then there were the docks, where Eustace worked, which were a prime target. The Surrey Docks had been badly hit in 1940, during the first raid of the Blitz. London was a horrible, depressing sight, and Lou was always glad to leave the city in order to get back to her relative calm in Rosehill.

They had a small Anderson shelter in the back garden at the house, but if Eustace was away for the night, Lou sometimes went to the new public air raid shelter on Green Lane. She'd rather be there than be home alone.

It was quite jolly down there at the public shelter - a bit like all the underground shelters in the city. Everyone took a bit of food and a flask or two of tea. Some people took books or magazines, some took their knitting. The kids had board games and some of the old men and women played cards. Young mothers tried to calm their fractious babies. Little children, thinking it was all a rather jolly game, ran around squealing and playing hide-and-seek between people's legs.

Lou rather enjoyed heading down there; everyone had a real Blitz spirit. They were all in the same boat, sheltering from Hitler and his thugs. They talked about their kids fighting overseas. They wept, laughed, and sang together. One of the old boys brought his accordion and another brought his mouth organ, so they belted out many of the same songs that their lads were singing in the trenches - "There'll Always Be an England," "The White Cliffs of Dover," "A Nightingale Sang in Berkeley Square," and "We'll Meet Again."

Eventually, by 1945, after two more long years, it was over. Germany was defeated at last, but at a huge cost. There had been so many lives lost, so much destruction, so much heartache. It would take many years for England to recover.

Ben eventually came home on a sunny day in March 1946, and Lou was sweeping the front doorstep with her back to the street.

"Hello, Mum."

Standing in front of her was a rather handsome young man, barely recognisable from the pale, skinny boy who had gone away five years earlier.

It took a while for her to stop shaking with emotion and excitement. She had almost given up hope of ever seeing her beloved son again.

"Oh, Ben. I can't believe you're home! And in one piece. Thank God."

She was holding him so tightly that he thought her arms would break.

"Come on, Mum. Let's get the kettle on, then we can sit down, have a nice cup of tea, and I can tell you all about it."

Lou couldn't take her eyes off of him. Her gorgeous, golden boy. He looked like such a man now. Just wait till his dad saw him!

They talked all afternoon. Ben told her about the wonders of Africa - the sun, sand, palm trees, and pineapples. The lovely local people with skin much darker than his. The friends he had made, the places he had seen. He didn't talk about all the carnage, the planes shot down, or the mates lost forever, buried in some foreign land. He didn't mention the ones who had been captured and kept as POWs. They certainly didn't talk about all the poor souls who had perished in the concentration camps; these were all topics for another day. Today was a day for rejoicing, for celebrating his return home.

There was no way of letting Eustace know the news; they had no telephone. If they sent a telegram to him at work, he probably would drop dead of a heart attack before he even opened it, assuming his boy had joined the list of those young men who would not be coming home alive.

"Eustace, close your eyes and come straight into the kitchen. I've got something to show you."

He groaned.

"Don't tell me those damn kids have kicked their ball over the fence and destroyed all my flowers again?"

"No, it's not that. Okay, you can open your eyes now."

As long as he lived, Eustace reckoned he would never forget that moment, that wonderful moment when he saw that his son had finally come home safely from war.

THE NEXT CHAPTER

Ben had been back in England for nearly two years. He missed the African sunshine and the constant blue skies, but he was glad to be home.

The joy on his parents' faces every time they looked at him for the first few weeks made the war fade away. He soon got used to being back in England, the country of his birth, the place his ancestors had lived for hundreds and hundreds of years.

However, he was a changed man. He did not suffer the deprivations of war in the same way others had. He had not fought in the trenches or kept the home fires burning in the Home Guard like his dad had, risking life and limb every time the air raid warnings sounded.

No, Ben's war had been different. He had witnessed young men - hundreds and hundreds of them - so excited to be trained as pilots. He saw young men imagining themselves impressing all the girls back home with tales of their exploits, only to perish, shot down by German bombers. Never to return to the country or the people they loved.

He went to visit Sid's mum.

"Oh Mum, it was so awful. She cried when I got there, cried all the time we were talking, and cried even more when I left. We talked a bit about Sid, then his brothers came inside. One of them is okay, a bit shell shocked, but not too bad. But the youngest one has lost one arm *and* one leg. It's going to be hard for him to get any work. Their Doreen's baby is a nice little thing, though. Apparently the Yank sent a few quid to her after the little one was born, but she hasn't heard from him since. Such a shame. She's a nice girl, I hope some bloke decides to marry her. She deserves a bit of happiness."

Ben's certificates from the technical college had all arrived while he was in South Africa, and his mum had stored them carefully in an old tin box.

"Every so often, while you were away, I used to take these out and look at them. Your dad and I are so proud of you, Ben. You're so clever, much brainier than either of us."

In truth, both Lou and Eustace were bright. They had just never had the opportunity to improve themselves through formal education. Growing up poor in Southwark meant life was all about day-to-day survival, earning enough money to keep a roof over your head and put food on the table. There was certainly nothing set aside for a fancy education.

Armed with his certificates and discharge papers from the Royal Air Force, Ben was able to secure a good job at Philips Electrical. Using the skills he had acquired in the military, he was well suited to work in the Amplifier and Radio Department at Century House on Shaftesbury Avenue, in the West End.

He enjoyed traveling up to London on the Tube every day. He didn't have to leave home as early as his dad did, so he got up at six, had a leisurely wash and shave, ate a nutritious breakfast that his mum lovingly prepared, and caught the bus to Morden station in time to get the 7:30am train.

Sometimes, if he was feeling particularly energetic, Ben would ride his bike and park it at the Underground station. He had bought his bike just after he was de-mobbed and loved it. It was his pride and joy; he had even joined a cycling club since being home. They met every weekend. Sometimes they just enjoyed short rides out to the country; other times they went on more adventurous trips, cycling all the way to the South Coast, Brighton, or Eastbourne.

The day the group cycled to Eastbourne, Ben had dragged them all to his Aunty Amber's house on the seafront. She was delighted to see all the fit, young men in her home and had supplied them with copious amounts of tea, sandwiches, and cake to give them energy for the return journey. Within the next month, the crew was planning to cycle all the way to the West Country. It would take a few days to get there, but it would be fun.

Lou and Eustace were delighted to see their boy getting on and enjoying his life. They didn't even mind that his bike took up all the room in their tiny hallway, although sometimes, Lou threatened to cart it up to his bedroom, out of the way.

"Don't be silly, Mum, that will just mean I have to lug it up and down the stairs every time I want to ride it. And if I need to do any repairs, oil the chain, or mend a puncture, it's much easier just to take it 'round the side gate to take care of it in the garden."

His mother rolled her eyes and his dad just chuckled. They were both so thrilled to have their boy home at last - they would agree to just about anything.

"We thought we might pop over to see the family in Whitstable in a couple of weeks. What do you think, Ben, do you want to come with us? Dad has to work till lunchtime on Saturday; we could always get the Tube to Victoria, meet him there, and then hop on the train to the coast. Aunty Ann and Grandma would love to see you... so would Arthur and his wife and kiddies. They've only seen you once since you got home."

The weekend in Whitstable was very successful. Everyone was delighted to see Ben and hear about his exploits during the war. Arthur's three small children sat, open-mouthed, as he told them of his adventures.

"Uncle Ben, did you see any whales? We're learning about them at school."

"I wish I could fly planes, see how good I am with this one?"

Ben had brought gifts for all of them - tins of biscuits for his aunty and Grandma and little balsa wood aeroplanes for the kids.

It had been great to catch up with his cousin again. They had shared so much as young boys, living in Peabody Buildings with all the family. Now, they were both grown men. Arthur was now a master boat builder, with a pretty wife and three adorable children.

"Do you think your Ben will get married and give you some grandchildren soon, Lou?"

Ann had always been very direct.

"Oh, Ann..." Grandma Jane interrupted, "...give the lad a chance! He's only just come back from the war. He probably needs to sow a few wild oats before he thinks about settling down."

"Okay, Mum. I was just thinking that our Lou isn't getting any younger. If she wants to be able to run around after her grandchildren like I have to do with this lot, Ben had better get a move on. Otherwise, she'll be too old."

AN ADDITION TO THE FAMILY

"**M**um, I've met someone."

It was early January of 1948. Ben had been home from war for almost two years now. It had been a busy, happy time for him and his family, filled with cycle rides, visits to the seaside, and weekends in London, staying with Astrid in Chelsea.

Ben was doing well at work, Lou was still enjoying working at the seed factory, and Eustace still travelled up to the docks every day. Life was ticking along nicely. Lou and Eustace still did their weekly trips to the cinema and looked forward to eating fish and chips on the way home. Occasionally Ben joined them - if there was a film on that he wanted to see - but mostly, it was just the two of them. This suited them very well; they looked forward to their Saturday nights out. It made them feel young again, wandering along, arm in arm. Sometimes they would even pop into The Rose for a quick drink before the film. He would have a pint of bitter and she usually chose a small sherry, or occasionally, a Babycham.

Ben had never brought a girl home before. In fact, his parents weren't even sure if he had ever had a serious girlfriend.

"I met her at Ernest's family Boxing Day party. In Battersea."

Ernest was a new friend, a chap Ben had met at the cycling club.

"I've invited her here for tea on Sunday. Is that okay?"

Sunday dawned, and Lou got up early to clean the house from top to bottom. By the time the men awoke, it was spotless. There was not a speck of dust in sight.

"Oh Mum, you needn't have bothered. Dot won't mind."

"Well, I'm not going to have anyone say I don't keep a nice house. Don't you dare, you two, get any of those crumbs on my nice, clean kitchen floor, or I'll be handing you both the dustpan and brush to clear it up."

Their guest arrived at three o'clock. Ben had gone up to the main road to meet her off the bus and Lou was peeping through the net curtains as the pair turned the corner onto Garendon Road.

"Ooh, she's very pretty, Eustace. A nice looking little thing. Well-dressed too."

"Mum, Dad, meet Dot. Let's get the kettle on, shall we?"

"Hello, pleased to meet you. Ben has told me so much about you both."

"Well, he hasn't told us much about you, love. Typical man! Eustace, you make the tea while I chat to this young lady. Ben, you can help your dad bring in the sandwiches and cake."

Lou had put a nice white cloth on the little table. It was a new table - well, new to them - that Eustace had picked up from a bloke in the pub. It fit perfectly into the space between the two old armchairs.

"So, come on love, tell me all about yourself."

Dot was a bit taken aback by the older woman's directness.

"Umm, well, I live in Morden, so not far away. I work up in town. I'm a tailoress. I started my apprenticeship before the war, then was lucky enough that they wanted me back after I was demobbed."

"Whereabouts in London do you work?"

"Just off Berwick Street. In Soho."

"I expect our Ben has told you that we're from Southwark. Cockneys, through and through."

"Oh yes, he did. My family comes from London, too. I was born in Camden Town."

"Oh, north of the river."

The men came into the room just in time to stop any further interrogation, but Lou couldn't contain herself for long.

"So, tell us about your family. Your mum and dad. How many brothers and sisters have you got? Or are you an only child, like our Ben? Mind you - he did have a little brother, a golden boy, apple of our eye. But he died just after his second birthday."

She went quiet for a few minutes after that. Talking about their little Denis always made her want to cry, even after all these years.

"Well, my dad works for Gieves and Hawkes and my brother John is with the London Underground, working as a clerk. He was a sailor during the war."

"And what about your mum, does she go to work?"

"No, my mum died when I was two. My dad did marry again, but my step-mum died too. I haven't had a mum since I was thirteen."

Dot sounded so forlorn. Lou's heart went out to her. Maybe, if her boy was serious about this young woman, she could end up filling some of the gap her mum had left behind. Lou could not imagine a world without her mum in it. Or having lived life without her grannies, for that matter.

"Have you got any other relatives? Aunties, uncles, grandparents?"

"I have got a lovely aunty and a couple of uncles, and one grandma. And a few cousins, too."

The afternoon went quite well. Ben walked Dot to the bus stop so she could catch her bus back to Morden.

"Do you think they liked me? Your mum asked so many questions. I got a bit flustered. Your dad was lovely, though."

He hugged her and gave her a quick kiss on the cheek.

"How could they fail to like you? I'm going to tell them tonight that I want to marry you."

"Oh, son. Are you sure? You've hardly known her five minutes. Don't you think you ought to play the field a bit more before you settle down?'

No Mum, I've made up my mind. She's the one for me.

That night, lying in Eustace's arms in the big feather bed, Lou brought it up again.

"What do you really think, love? Is she the right girl for him? She seems alright. Maybe a bit stuck up though? I saw her face when I said we were Cockneys through and through... I think she feels a bit superior."

"Oh Lou, give the poor girl a chance. She seemed lovely. I pity anyone who tries to take on our Ben; no one is ever going to be good enough for our boy, according to you!"

The wedding took place the following spring, on a chilly day in early March. It was held in Dot's local parish, St. Lawrence.

The little church was packed. Everyone had come down to Morden for the wedding.

Lou and Eustace sat in the front pew on the right-hand side and Lou's mum, Granny Jane, sat beside them. In the row behind them were Ben's Aunty Ann and her husband, Arthur, his wife, and their three children.

The next row held Astrid, Amber and Fred, and their two girls. Behind them were Alice and Amy and their families. There were a few folks from Southwark and several of Ben's friends from the cycling club.

Standing at the front, waiting for the bride to arrive, was a rather nervous Ben. His friend and cycling mate, Ernest, stood with him as his best man. He was in charge of the ring and Ben's emotions.

"It's alright, mate. She'll be here soon. She's not going to ditch you at the altar - not now you've bought her her own bike!"

The two young men burst out laughing and the elderly vicar glared at them. This was supposed to be a serious event, not some music hall turn!

On the other side of the aisle sat Dot's family and friends. Her brother John and his wife Jean were in the front row, and there was a space next to them where Dot's father would sit. Behind were her Aunty Rose, Uncle Cyril, and grandmother. Most of the other rows were filled with family and friends, although Lou was secretly pleased to see that their side - the groom's side - was busier. Obviously, her Ben was more popular than his bride.

Suddenly, the little church was filled with the sound of the organ playing Mendelssohn's "Wedding March" and her new daughter-in-law, on the arm of her father, Valentine George, came down the aisle towards them.

She had to admit that the girl looked very beautiful today. Pale and rather shy, but very beautiful.

Dot was wearing a lovely white satin dress with a sweetheart neckline and long sleeves. At the bottom of each sleeve and all down the back of the long dress were tiny covered buttons, made from matching satin. The satin fabric had a watermark pattern. It was an exquisite dress, a fine piece of tailoring and Lou was impressed. Her new daughter-in-law was obviously a very good tailor. She knew that she had sewn every stitch on the dress herself, had even made the matching veil and the two bridesmaids dresses - all carefully sewn by hand. Such a lot of work!

Lou smiled as the bride passed her and Dot gave a weak smile back. She became more relaxed as she finally reached her husband-to-be. Ben gave her hand a little squeeze to reassure her before they both turned to face the vicar.

"Dearly beloved, we are gathered here today, in the presence of God, to celebrate the marriage of Benjamin and Doris - although I think you all know them better as Ben and Dot!"

Lou cried through most of the service. Even Eustace looked a bit tearful at times, and they both knew they were thinking about their own wedding on Christmas Eve of 1913, thinking back to when they exchanged their own vows in the church in Southwark. What a lot had happened since then.

Now it was 1949. The war had been over for nearly four years, and life was beginning to get back to normal. Of course, there was still a lot of destruction everywhere. Houses and businesses had been ruined and on every corner there seemed to be a bombsite. At the same time though, people were beginning to feel optimistic. Clothes rationing had just ended; at last, they would be able to pop into the shops to buy something *new*, rather than having to "make do and mend." They had all felt so drab during the long war years, it was finally time to enjoy a bit of colour and style again.

At Ben's wedding, Lou and her sisters flaunted the "New Look," a wonderful change from the utility clothing everyone had been forced to wear for the last few years. Now, they could buy material and patterns again, or go to the shops and get something ready-made.

How splendid they had all looked. Of course, you couldn't see their pretty flowery dresses because they were all covered up by thick winter coats they had been forced to wear. Everyone wanted to be protected from the chilly spring breeze. However, even the coats were special - all brand new. They were made from wool, some plain, some tweed, and all with nipped waists and full, billowing skirts that hung just below the calves. Most of the coats were fairly plain, but beautifully tailored. Ann had black velvet lapels on her grey coat with a matching velvet hat that was trimmed with grey and purple flowers. Astrid wore a very simple coat in a sensible, serviceable dark colour. Amber, of course, tried to outdo them all. Her coat was made of the softest wool, in a shade of pale lavender, and it was trimmed on the collar, cuffs, and hemline with grey fur.

Granny Jane, the shortest of them all, looked very smart in her navy blue coat and matching navy velvet collar, thick navy stockings, and wide-brimmed hat, trimmed with pink and cream flowers.

Lou felt a bit like the ugly sister that day. She always felt like that around her tall and beautiful older sisters; somehow, they still made her feel like a kid.

"Nice coat, Lou. It's a shame you didn't get the dressmaker to add a bit of trim to it, though. Tweed can be a bit shabby - a bit ordinary without something to dress it up a bit."

She felt uncomfortable all through the church service and all through posing for photographs outside in the churchyard. It was only when they got back to The Rose for the reception and she took her coat off that she began to feel better.

"Nice dress, Lou. You should wear green more often, it suits you."

Eustace could tell she was a bit unhappy. It wasn't just the emotion of seeing her boy get wed, he could tell her sisters had upset her.

"Maybe I should have got a brighter coat? I just thought this would be a bit more practical since it is plainish... a bit more suitable for everyday wear and not just for the wedding."

His heart went out to his wife. He wished he earnt enough money so that she could have really splashed out, like her sister Amber had obviously done. He bet Amber never wore that flashy lavender-coloured thing just to go shopping!

Eustace knew that Lou had scrimped on the weekly shopping lately - buying tins of Spam instead of nice, juicy ham - just so she could save a few pennies to help with the wedding costs.

And now, their new daughter-in-law was going to move in with them, into Ben's bedroom. There just weren't enough places around for all the young ones to move into - so much housing stock had been destroyed in the war. Lots of young married couples were having to give up their dreams for their first married home, and instead move in with their mums and dads for the time being. Eustace just hoped it was all going to work out okay. Dot seemed like a nice girl, but as his old mum had always said, *"It's not wise to have two women in the house who both think they're in charge... especially in the kitchen!"*

Truthfully, it was a shame they hadn't been able to move into Dot's dad's place. He knew that was what she had really wanted, but unfortunately, her brother and his wife had beaten them to it, having moved in after their wedding late last year. Her new sister-in-law had told Dot that as soon as she moved out, they were taking over her bedroom for the new baby they were expecting.

Dot's father, Valentine George, was obviously upset about it. He would much rather have shared his home with his own daughter than with some random woman his son had decided to marry, but he wasn't strong enough to stand up for himself or her. He had always been too much of a soft touch.

Eustace had really enjoyed chatting to old Valentine George at the wedding reception. They had compared notes about their childhoods - even though they had grown up on opposite sides of the river, they were both Londoners, through and through. During their adult lives, they had both moved out to the country somewhat unwillingly, pushed into doing so by strong, assertive wives. They also both liked the occasional pint and read the newspapers avidly.

"In further news..." Shortly after the wedding, Eustace sat at the kitchen table, reading the newspaper.

"...Next month they are apparently going to sign the North Atlantic Treaty, creating something called NATO, which is, according to Prime Minister Clement Attlee, is going to create 'peace with all peoples and all governments.'" Eustace scoffed when they heard that on the radio the day before.

"What a load of old codswallop. They've said that before and they'll say it again. I don't believe there'll ever truly be world peace; there's too many power hungry men like Hitler out there."

"I heard there's going to be a dockers' strike next week. Is that true, Dad? What are you lot hoping to achieve by doing that? You know they'll just bring in the Army to unload all the stuff at the docks; they're not just going to let it all pile up while you lot fight for a few extra quid."

Eustace was a staunch union man, as were most of his fellow dockers. Their work was undeniably hard and they didn't feel they were valued or recompensed enough.

"Ben, until you've done a hard day's work, lugging enormous, heavy crates from one end of the docks to another, I don't reckon you're in any position to judge. You just go to work every day in your smart clothes; the worst that happens while you're sitting at your comfy workbench building radios, or whatever it is you do, is you spill a bit of ink on your clean, white shirt."

Ben blushed. His dad was right. Thanks to the sacrifices both his parents had made, he had never had to work as hard as his dad did - never had to get up at the crack of dawn every day to travel miles to a job that would wreck a lesser man.

"Sorry, Dad. I really do appreciate everything you do for me. I know it isn't easy having me and Dot live here. It's a bit of a squash for us all, but at least we're out all day. You only have to put up with us on weekends, really."

By the time the new decade started in 1950, everyone was used to the shared living situation. In truth, it wasn't what any of them would have chosen, but, having had no option, they were trying to make the best of it.

"I just feel that she always looks down on us a bit, what with you being a docker and me working down at the factory. But she doesn't understand that I *love* factory work. I guess it's in my blood. Loads of my ancestors did factory work. I can remember, when I was little, seeing all the Bryant and May Match girls pouring out of the factory gates at home-time.

I was so envious; I thought they looked wonderful. I wanted to be one of them when I grew up, but Mum and Dad wouldn't let me. They said the match factory was a dreadful place to work, so I ended up at the leather place instead."

In early 1951, nearly two years after Ben and Dot's wedding, Ben gave his parents some news.

When Dot got home that evening, tired after a long day at work and just wanting to get inside, take her shoes off, have a nice cup of tea, and maybe go to bed early, she was greeted at the front door by her mother-in-law. She had barely got in the door when the older woman spoke.

"So, I hear you're pregnant."

As they lay in bed that night, she sobbed in Ben's arms.

"Your mum hates me, I know she does. She didn't even say congratulations about the baby. She just said 'Oh, I hear you're pregnant.' Made me feel like some little kid who'd got into trouble."

In the bedroom opposite, another conversation was taking place.

"Maybe you should just apologise to the girl. You did sound a bit harsh. Not the response she was expecting. Not like an excited Granny. No wonder she was upset."

"Well, I was just a bit surprised. I didn't even know they were trying for a baby. I thought Ben said that 'cos of a few problems she'd had when she was a youngster, she probably wouldn't be able to have kids of her own. He told me the other week that they'd been thinking about adoption instead. So it was a bit of a shock, that's all."

"I know, love. But I really do think you should apologise to the girl for being so rude. Don't forget, she hasn't got a mum or a sister, and I don't think she gets on too well with that hard faced sister-in-law of hers."

Sadly, Lou never apologised to Dot. Like all things left unsaid in life, the resentment began to fester.

By the time baby Ann was born, four months later, the two women were barely talking. They exchanged pleasantries, even went shopping together a few times to buy things for the baby, but when Eustace or Ben were not around, they hardly said a word to each other.

Dot was home all day with the baby. She was forced to give up her job after giving birth and she rather resented it. She had loved traveling up to the city every day, loved the camaraderie of the little sewing room, and loved earning her own money. She loved feeling like an independent woman.

Despite all the drama, they all adored baby Ann. She was a pretty, blonde-haired little thing, the apple of everyone's eye.

Ben was a great father. He took his girl on long walks - at first in her pram, then while holding her hand tightly after she learnt to toddle along on her own little feet.

Ann was a joy to them all, whether she was singing nursery rhymes at the top of her lungs, washing and pegging out her dollies' clothes on the line, helping Eustace to pick flowers from the garden to go on the mantelpiece, or dressing up for the coronation's fancy dress party that was held on the Green. When she won second prize, wearing a lovely little dress that Dot had made from crepe paper, they were all thrilled.

Three and a half years later, everything changed. By this point, they were used to sharing the house. It was not ideal for any of them, but they made do.

Ben's bike - which he had always parked in the narrow hallway, much to Lou's annoyance - had been relegated upstairs to his old bedroom. The bedroom he now shared with his wife and daughter. What with the baby's cot, their bed, and the small wooden wardrobe, it was rather a squeeze in there. Dot often sat on the bed and daydreamed about a day, probably way in the future, if ever, when they would have a place of their own. She dreamt of a place where she could shut the front door, knowing her mother-in-law was not in the next room.

Dot didn't hate Lou, she just didn't like her very much. Especially since the time she had spoken to her so rudely when she found out Dot was pregnant. How on earth was the old battle axe going to react to the latest news?

"By the way Mum, we're going to have another baby. But don't worry, Dot's managed to get us on the housing list. They reckon they might be able to offer us a place before the new baby arrives!"

Lou blushed. She knew she hadn't behaved very well last time. If only she could turn back the clock; she really would have liked a better relationship with her daughter-in-law.

By the time the second little girl was born five months later, Ben and Dot were installed in a brand new council house some twelve miles away from Rosehill.

"I wish they hadn't gone so far. I suppose we're only going to be able to see the little 'uns at weekends. I'll miss having little Ann around; she was always such good company. The house just doesn't feel the same without her running around, singing all over the place. What on earth are we going to do with ourselves, Eustace, now our boy's gone, too?"

Lou wished with all her heart that things had happened differently, that her daughter-in-law hadn't been so keen to get away from them.

"Maybe we were both a bit at fault. Two different generations of women, with different ideas. Maybe I should have tried a bit harder. One day, years ago now, Astrid told me I was being too hard on the girl. She said I should remember that Dot had never had a mum or sisters around, so she didn't understand that one could be a bit direct - or even say something a bit nasty - and know their mum and sisters would always forgive them. I don't think she ever really forgave me for not showing I was excited when she was expecting little Ann. And now it's too late. They've all gone."

She burst into tears and Eustace held her tightly while she sobbed. He wondered how many times, in the forty-two years they'd been married, he had had to hold her like this. His wonderful, feisty wife.

"Oh, Eustace, do you think there's anything I can do to make it better? I don't want to lose my boy - or my grandchildren."

They tried very hard. They would often get the bus on the weekends to visit Ben and his little family at their new home in the country.

The visits were often tense. It was obvious that Dot didn't really want them there - didn't really want them to be part of her children's lives, actually.

The family rarely came to visit Lou and Eustace at Rosehill.

Ben was a good son, so he dropped in religiously on his own every Saturday afternoon when he finished work. He would stay just an hour or so, long enough to check they were both okay.

"Why doesn't Dot bring the children over to see us one day during the school holidays? They could even stay the night; you could come after work and we could babysit. Then you and Dot could have a night off, maybe go to the pictures or something! You could even take her up to town, I bet she misses going up there every day. It must be hard for her, stuck out there in the country all day long with just the little ones to talk to while you're at work."

For the next few years, Lou and Eustace only saw their grandchildren occasionally. They would get the bus, then walk the twenty minutes or so to the little two-bedroom brick house on the new estate. Sometimes, Eustace would take Dot a few flowers from his garden. The kids seemed pleased to see them, especially when their granddad slipped a shiny half crown into each of their hands as he left. By now there were four of them - three girls and one boy - so it was getting a bit expensive. Ben would walk them to the bus stop when the visits were over; he loved his parents dearly and was always glad to see them. After every visit, Lou cried all the way home on the bus.

Needing something else to fill the gaps in their lives, they started going on coach trips. Just little getaways to the seaside at first - a few days in Torquay, Brighton, or Hastings. They loved the seaside and would spend hours lying in rented deck chairs, just soaking up the sun.

Once Eustace retired, after a lifetime on the docks, they travelled further afield - to the Continent. They visited Copenhagen, Venice, Amsterdam, and even to Germany, where they were astonished that a country with so much beauty and so many majestic castles could have produced a son as infamous as Adolph Hitler.

Lou and Eustace both loved the ambience of a coach holiday. There were plenty of fellow passengers to make friends with, no foreign languages to worry about (the tour guide took care of all that), and the chance to see a bit of the world. Eustace, of course, had seen much of it before when he was a young sailor, but to Lou, it was all so fresh and so exciting.

"Oh, Eustace, I wish we'd done this years ago. Look at us, two kids from Southwark, living the high life!"

The years ticked by as years always do, and nothing much changed. The old couple still went on coach trips, adding Switzerland, Austria, and the Italian Riviera to their list of visited places. They sent postcards from every trip to their grandchildren - children they hardly saw because their mother didn't like her in-laws much.

"Ben, how are the children? We do miss them. I wish you could bring them to see us sometimes. Bet they're all getting really big now."

Lou knew that Dot often took them down to Morden to see *her* family. Morden, just ten minutes away - actually on the same bus route. But she almost never came to see them.

"Actually, Mum, we'll be down at Morden for Christmas. I'll see if Dot will let me bring the kids over then."

He was as good as his word. On Boxing Day afternoon, they all arrived. All of them except Dot.

"Oh, sorry, she had to stay behind to help Jean make some more sausage rolls and mince pies. This lot of gluttons already got through the first batch Jean made. She did send you both her love, though."

"Oh, Dad, it wasn't just us. You ate loads of them, too. Aunty Jean kept telling you off, but we saw you sneaking into the kitchen to get more"

It was true. Ben's eldest daughter, Ann, was absolutely right. He was very partial to a nice sausage roll!

Lou looked across the room to where her eldest granddaughter was sitting at the table, helping the smallest one of her siblings colour in the new colouring book her grandparents had given her. It was hard to believe this was the same little girl who had lived here in this house, sharing their home until she was three and a half years old. She had turned into a fine young woman; she was nineteen now and had just announced that she was getting married next year - to a young man her grandparents had never met.

Eustace stayed in the house, enjoying entertaining his grandchildren with stories of his life growing up in Southwark, while Ben and Lou had wandered out to the garden to have a private chat.

"Granddad, is it true that our dad used to be good at marbles? He reckons he was the champion of Peabody Buildings."

"Granddad, is it really true that Nanny has seen *The Sound of Music* sixteen times?"

Lou heard the sound of their laughter.

"Sixteen times? How on earth could anyone see it sixteen times?"

"Well, the first time I went with her. I liked it well enough but didn't really want to go and see it again the next week, so she went on her own. Then she said she was going again and again, until finally she said she'd seen it enough to know all the songs by heart. When she comes in from the garden, I bet we could get her to sing some of them, if you'd like."

"Ben, what do you *really* think about Ann getting married so young? Is he suitable? What does he do? Will he be good to her, do you think? She's such a sweet little thing; I'd hate to think of anyone taking advantage of her."

"Oh, Mum. We're not really happy about it all. Dot is beside herself, says he's all wrong for our girl and that she didn't like him the minute she set eyes on him. I'm not sure if that really means he's no good or not. I'm just worried that she's too young. She's booked the wedding for exactly two weeks after her 20th birthday. She's paying for it all herself - she knows we can't afford a big fancy wedding. She's managed to save quite a bit of money, having worked in the bank now for the four years since she left school. But I'd be lying if I said I wasn't worried. We don't really know much about him or his family at all."

"Didn't you try to stop her, to talk her out of it? At least for a couple more years?"

Oh, Mum, you know our girl. She's feisty, just like you are. The more we tried to stop her, the more determined she got. I guess we'll just have to cross our fingers and hope it works out. At least we'll be there to pick up the pieces if it doesn't."

THE FINAL YEARS

In December 1977, six years after their granddaughter's wedding and just a week before his and Lou's 65th wedding anniversary, Eustace died.

They had been sitting in their armchairs having a little nap after lunch, and he never woke up.

Lou had sat with him for an hour holding his cold hand, tears pouring down her old, wrinkled face.

"Oh, love, why did you have to go? How am I ever going to go on without you? I don't think I can."

The next door neighbour phoned Ben at work and he came straight away.

"How did you know to go 'round there?"

Ben knew that his mum and the lady next door were friendly, but thought they were just on nodding terms. Lou had never felt the need for many female friends; she had always had her Eustace and he had been enough.

"Oh, lad. I'd just nodded off in the armchair and I suddenly heard this wailing coming from next door. I didn't take much notice at first, thought maybe your mum and dad just had the television on really loud, then it got worse. Much worse, like howling, really. A really raw, animal kind of sound. So I popped 'round and the front door wasn't locked. I knocked but there was no answer, so I just let myself in. Then I found her like this. She won't let go of him. I didn't know what to do, but I found your work number on the board in the kitchen so I rang you. I'm sorry, lad. Your dad was a nice old gent - always very polite."

Lou sat by his body until the doctor... and then the undertakers... came. The doctor spoke to her gently.

"I'm so sorry, Lou. It was a massive heart attack. Nothing you or I could have done to stop it. It was just his time, I'm afraid. Still, he had a good innings. Not many men who have worked as hard as he did make it to 88.

The funeral was heartbreaking. No one could bear to watch the little old lady, who was head to toe in black mourning clothes, as she followed the coffin that carried her beloved husband out to the graveyard. She had to be held tightly by her son so she would not jump into the empty grave herself.

"Oh, Ben. I just want to go in there with him. What am I going to do without him? I don't think I can go on."

But of course, Lou did go on - for another seven lonely years.

She hated every day without her Eustace.

"Oh, Ann, love, I just can't bear it. Your granddad was such a lovely man - the only man I ever loved. I just hate living without him."

Young Ann had popped in to see her.

"I can't sleep in our bed. It's so big and lonely without him, so I've moved into your dad's old bedroom - the one you used to sleep in when you were tiny and you all lived with us.

Your Aunty Astrid has offered for me to go and live with her in Chelsea and Ann's always harping on about her spare room in Whitstable, but I can't face moving. All my happy memories of your granddad are here."

The girl stroked her grandmother's hand gently, noticing the age spots and wrinkles and silently hoping this would never happen to her.

"I heard Mum say to Dad the other day that perhaps you should go and live with them. What do you think?"

Lou gave a sad little smile. This girl was so kind, so sweet. It was a thoughtful suggestion from her daughter-in-law, but she knew Dot's heart probably wasn't in it. She was asking out of duty, not love.

"What did your dad say?" For a fleeting moment, Lou had a vision of spending the rest of her days surrounded by her son and his loving family. But Ann's next words squashed that dream.

"Dad said it probably wasn't a good idea. He said that he would be out at work all day, the kids would be at school, and it would just be more work and another mouth to feed. He said he thought you'd be much happier staying where you are."

Lou lived alone for another seven years. Seven long years of missing her Eustace and wishing she could hurry up and die so she could join him in the cemetery.

She became a little frail towards the end, so Ben organised some home help - people to come in and help her clean the house and prepare the odd meal here and there.

Unfortunately the people the agency sent were not always honest; gradually, her little collection of gold jewellery - the dainty watches, bracelets, and rings that Eustace had bought her on their foreign trips - started to disappear. Lou began hiding precious things under a loose floorboard in the kitchen, even wrapping a few old family photographs in newspaper: pictures from family weddings and two cherished photos of her little Dennis, her golden boy.

At the grand age of 94, Lou died quietly and with dignity, falling asleep in her own bed, in her own house. For some reason, on that last night she had decided to be brave. She went back into the bedroom she had shared for so many years with her one true love. She climbed into the big, soft feather bed, enjoying the smell of the fresh lavender sheets. She kissed her photo of Eustace, as she had done every night since he died, and then closed her eyes. At last she slept - the best sleep she had had in years.

THE END

REFERENCES

PRINCESS MARY'S GIFT BOOK
An anthology, published in 1914 by Hodder and Stoughton.

SWALLOWS AND AMAZONS
A children's novel by Arthur Ransome, published in 1930.

DOWN AND OUT IN PARIS AND LONDON
By George Orwell, published in 1933

THE MENTAL HEALTH TREATMENT ACT, 1930

Did you enjoy this book? If so, please leave me a review.
I would be delighted to hear from you!

Meet me on my website: www.patbackley.com

AUTHOR BIOGRAPHY

Pat Backley is an English woman who, at the age of 59, decided to become a Kiwi.

She now lives in New Zealand; when not writing, she loves to travel the world (Covid permitting!). She particularly loves spending time in Fiji with her beloved extended Fijian family. She also gardens, paints, reads, and loves activities like interior design, walks on the beach, and socialising.

In short, Pat now lives an ideal existence, but it hasn't always been easy (as her memoirs **FROM THERE TO HERE, WITH AN AWFUL LOT IN BETWEEN** will explain).

Pat's other books are:

DAISY (published 2020)
THE SECOND DAISY (published 2021)
FROM THERE TO HERE.,WITH AN AWFUL LOT IN BETWEEN (published 2021)
SEVENTY YEARS WORTH OF TRAVEL (published 2022)

VALENTINE GEORGE (published 2022)

She has also co-authored two anthologies: A best selling coffee table book entitled, **THE WARRIOR WOMEN PROJECT: A SISTERHOOD OF IMMIGRANT WOMEN**, and **THE RELATABLE VOICES,** a collection of short stories.

To learn more about these and her upcoming books, visit her website: **www.patbackley.com**